DISASTERS
ACROSS CANADA

AMAZING STORIES®

DISASTERS ACROSS CANADA

Bravery in the Face of Danger and Destruction

HISTORY/HUMAN INTEREST

by Art Montague

PUBLISHED BY ALTITUDE PUBLISHING CANADA LTD.
1500 Railway Avenue, Canmore, Alberta T1W 1P6
www.amazingstories.ca
1-800-957-6888

Copyright 2006 © Art Montague
All rights reserved
First published 2006

Extreme care has been taken to ensure that all information presented in
this book is accurate and up to date. Neither the author nor the
publisher can be held responsible for any errors.

Publisher	Stephen Hutchings
Associate Publisher	Kara Turner
Editors	Megan Lappi and Lori Burwash
Digital Photo Colouring	Bryan Pezzi

We acknowledge the financial support of the Government
of Canada through the Book Publishing Industry Development
Program (BPIDP) for our publishing activities.

Altitude GreenTree Program
Altitude Publishing will plant twice as many trees as were used
in the manufacturing of this product.

National Library of Canada Cataloguing in Publication Data

CIP data available from the publisher upon request.
ISBN 1-55439-004-4

Amazing Stories® is a registered trademark of Altitude Publishing Canada Ltd.

Printed and bound in Canada by Friesens
2 4 6 8 9 7 5 3 1

To Canada's courageous first responders,
past and present.

Contents

Prologue

Beyond its harbours, some would argue, the St. Lawrence River is no place for Sunday sailors. The river's currents clash constantly as outflow from the Great Lakes struggles against incoming frigid tides from the North Atlantic. Its dark, deceptive surface cloaks lurking rocks and is often battened by bone-chilling, blinding fog lasting days or, sometimes, only a few minutes. Despite these hazards, the St. Lawrence River's shipping lanes are among the busiest in North America, crowded with the commerce of the world's nations.

In 1914, the SS Storstad *was part of this commerce. Inbound from Nova Scotia, she was an unspectacular workaday collier ship carrying 9000 tons of coal consigned for Montreal.*

The 3600-ton Storstad *churned resolutely through the water on a tight schedule driven by the demands of the steel industry's blazing Bessemers and coal furnaces in homes across Canada. The captain and crew expected the trip to be uneventful, as routine as a hundred others that had preceded it.*

By 1:30 a.m., the Storstad's *captain, Thomas Andersen, had retired to his cabin. He left orders with his veteran helmsman, First Officer Alfred Tuftenes, to wake him if anything untoward occurred or, barring that, when the* Storstad *arrived off Father Point, Quebec, to take aboard a pilot.*

The night sky was clear, the river smooth, the wind no more than a light breeze. Then First Officer Tuftenes spotted the lights of another ship about 9.5 kilometres away and manoeuvred to pass it. It appeared to Tuftenes that the unknown ship did the same. Suddenly a fog bank closed vision, sealing the Storstad *into the night. However, given what he'd seen, Tuftenes was confident the ships would safely pass each other. The voyage remained routine.*

Twenty minutes later, Tuftenes was horrified to see the unmistakable lights of a massive passenger liner looming out of the fog 30 metres dead ahead. One of the greatest Canadian marine disasters of all time was about to happen.

Chapter 1
Dangerous Waters

C anada is bound on three sides by oceans and boasts the longest coastline in the world. In addition, the country has more bodies of freshwater — lakes and rivers — than any other nation in the world. Beneficial and often beautiful, Canada's waters can also be extremely dangerous to the ships that sail on them.

The Tragic *Empress*
The passenger liner *Empress of Ireland* was a jewel in the Canadian Pacific Steamship Company's proud ocean passenger fleet. Bound for Liverpool, England, on the afternoon of May 28, 1914, her boarding passengers must have been comforted when they saw the 184-metre-long queen of the sea abutting the pier on the Quebec City waterfront.

Clean-lined and sparkling, the ship exuded the prospect of warm Edwardian splendour, convivial company, and safe passage. Coloured streamers drifted down from the upper decks. On the pier, playing music while it waited to board, was the 40-member Salvation Army Band.

At 4:30 that afternoon, the *Empress*'s crew cast off her lines and the ship steamed gracefully into the St. Lawrence River's mainstream with 1057 passengers on board.

Dinner on the *Empress* that evening was the first formal social gathering of the passengers. Spotless linen tablecloths and napkins, shimmering silverware, and the steamship line's famous "invisible" service created an ambience in the dining rooms that would have lent gourmet succulence to a blue plate special. The evening vibrated with the passengers' excitement. For many, this was their first sea voyage, and, for all, there was the thrill of setting off on a transatlantic adventure.

The largest single contingent of passengers was 167 Canadian Salvation Army members and their families, heading to a conference in London. Already the Salvationists had provided fellow passengers the prospect of a trip filled with music and cheer. After dinner, passengers strolled the decks or retired early to their cabins. Some gentlemen lingered in the smoking rooms and library to savour a nightcap and a cigar, while the ladies relaxed in the music room or other salons furnished exclusively for their comfort.

Later, the *Empress* paused briefly at Rimouski on the

river's south shore to pick up mail and drop her pilot, then she continued on. Most passengers were unaware of the stop, already in bed for the night.

At about 1:30 a.m., *Empress* captain Henry Kendall spotted the *Storstad*. In the fog, Kendall ordered his ship to a full stop, assuming the approaching *Storstad* would safely clear him. Stock-still, the *Empress* idled while the *Storstad* powered over the river.

Just before 2 a.m., unable to sleep and perhaps wanting a breath of fresh air, *Empress* passenger John Smart poked his head out of his cabin porthole. This was his first night on the water, and he was restless with the anticipation of his voyage to England.

Coincidentally, another passenger, George Fowler, did the same. Both men saw the *Storstad* emerge out of the fog like a malevolent leviathan. "Almost close enough to touch," Fowler later said. Both men also felt the *Storstad* slice deeply into their ship — it penetrated 31 metres through the *Empress's* 22-millimetre-thick hull, more like a sheet of tissue than a bulwark. Although the *Empress* was more than three times the size of the *Storstad*, the collier ship was a workhorse, built to voyage in all kinds of weather and break through ice.

After the collision, both ships were carried apart by their momentum, leaving the passenger liner with a gaping 107-metre hole below her waterline, reaching deep into her heart — the boiler rooms.

Ironically, minutes after the collision, the fog bank lifted and the clear night sky revealed the horrific scene to the *Storstad* crew. The weight of water rushing into her bowels had already rolled the *Empress* onto her side, her twin funnels almost touching the river. Within 14 minutes, the *Empress* had slid beneath the river, sinking 39 metres to a thick bed of silt on the bottom.

In 1914, radar had not yet been invented, but the *Empress* had plenty of life jackets and lifeboats. Based on lessons learned from the sinking of the *Titanic* only two years earlier, the *Empress* was fitted with state-of-the-art safety features. Unfortunately, the manner in which the ship rolled and the speed at which she sank prevented the use of most of these features.

In bed for the night, many passengers were trapped in their cabins. Of those who could reach the corridors, many were fatally disoriented by the roll of the ship and torrent of water. Others, whose cabins opened directly onto the deck, escaped, only to instantly lose their balance and slide down the near-vertical deck into the river.

The *Storstad* crew laboured for a long time rescuing survivors, then spent many more hours recovering bodies. Two other smaller ships also helped with the rescue, one staying at the scene well into the next day before giving up and returning to Rimouski.

John Fowler and George Smart were rescued by the *Storstad* crew. Captain Kendall, thrown into the river when the *Empress* rolled, was among the first rescued and taken aboard the *Storstad*. On the ship's deck, he confronted Captain Andersen. "Sir," he accused, "you have sunk my ship!"

Another passenger, George Crellin, survived because he was a strong swimmer. Swimming for a lifeboat, he encountered a child, Florence Barbour, floundering helplessly in the oil-slicked water. Crellin persuaded the girl to climb on his back. When her tiny arms were tight around his neck, he swam on. After the two were rescued, he learned that Florence was now an orphan. She had lost her mother and sister in the sinking and her father had died the previous year. Crellin took her into his home, where he and his wife raised her.

Of the 167 Salvationists, only 33 survived; of 138 children, only 4. In total, 1012 people perished in the worst marine disaster in Canadian history. With 840 passenger fatalities, the sinking of the *Empress of Ireland* was more deadly than the *Titanic*'s sinking.

While culpability was never resolved, the point is incidental in the face of the simple acts of heroism that occurred after the collision: life jackets were given up to non-swimmers, places were yielded in already overcrowded lifeboats, and swimmers helped others to safety before they themselves sank into the river.

Sadly, tragedy soon followed tragedy. Less than a month after the *Empress* sank, World War I started.

The Demise of the *Princess Sophia*

Shipping along Canada's Pacific Northwest coast would be far riskier if not for the Inside Passage. By 1918, this waterway stretching from Alaska to Vancouver and west along the east coasts of Vancouver Island and the Queen Charlotte Islands was well mapped and the currents well defined. The passage usually provided protection to ships from storms tearing in from the Pacific Ocean, but at times it was a frenzied funnel for hurricane-force storms raging out of the north.

During the winter, the passage closed, which explained why the Canadian Pacific steamship *Princess Sophia* was at capacity when she departed Skagway, Alaska, for Vancouver in late October 1918 — her last trip before winter.

Every captain, navigator, and ship's pilot who travelled the Inside Passage knew of Vanderbilt Reef. Although the reef was marked with a buoy, without lights, the buoy was useless at night, particularly during a storm. At 11 p.m. on October 24, during a sudden early winter blizzard, the *Sophia*, with 343 passengers and crew aboard, slammed aground the reef. The *Sophia* was caught in a trough of rock, as if in a cradle from which she might eventually float free.

Although the ship's shuddering stop created disarray on board, initial panic was minimal and fleeting. Captain Leonard Locke immediately ordered a damage assessment, which determined that while there was a hole in the hull, the ship wasn't taking on water — not so dangerous a situation as to threaten seaworthiness.

Beyond a few bruises and some minor shaking about, no passengers or crew were injured. With a list of only about five percent, the ship was still on a relatively even keel. Captain Locke had his radio operator, David Robinson, request assistance from Juneau, Alaska, about 64 kilometres away, and from Skagway, more than 100 kilometres away. The storm continued throughout the night, every wave grating the *Sophia* against the rocks.

By dawn, several small rescue ships were on the scene. Locke's intention was to disembark the passengers and attempt to float his ship free on the high tide at about 5 that morning. However, rescue ships could approach within only 180 metres of the *Sophia*. They were within clear sight, but due to stormy seas and the reef's threatening rocks, lifeboats were required for any rescue. Unfortunately, the sea was so rough that even they could not be put into the water.

High tide came and went, and the *Sophia* stayed wedged on the reef. Throughout the day, the sea remained too rough to launch lifeboats from either the *Sophia* or the rescue boats, which still stood aside waiting for a lull in the turbulence.

As the afternoon wore on, the storm's intensity increased. Wind gusts were estimated at 160 kilometres per hour. Fearing for the safety of the rescue ships, several of which were small fishing vessels, and believing his own position secure, Captain Locke advised them to seek shelter from the storm, which they did. They could return if the storm subsided during the night or in the morning.

The rescue ships were barely alee of the storm at 4:50 p.m. when a wireless message came from the *Sophia.* "Ship foundering on reef. Come at once!"

Half an hour later, David Robinson radioed a final desperate message: "For God's sake, hurry. The water is coming in my room." He would have been in the pilot house, which was situated well above the waterline.

By then, the storm was a full blow, a gale and blizzard as fierce as any that had ever torn down the Inside Passage. The rescue ships, which had barely made safe harbour, had no choice but to wait out the storm; to have ventured back into the seething channel would have meant certain destruction.

Rescue crews slept little that night. The men listened for a lull in the wind, waited for a softening of the waves rocking their ships — any indication from the weather and the sea that they could make a rescue attempt. As they waited, they hoped and prayed that the people on the *Sophia* could somehow make it through the night. These were veteran seamen who had themselves experienced the power of the Inside Passage storms. They knew that every passing minute could echo a death knell.

The storm lessened only a little by morning. One of the rescue captains, standing on an island three kilometres from the reef, could see nothing except about six metres of the *Sophia's* mainmast thrust above the water.

At 8:30 that morning, still bucking heavy seas and snow, the rescue ships were finally able to return to the scene. They were guided by the *Sophia*'s mast — a still visible sentinel of disaster. Rescuers searched the sea and shoreline for three hours before finding the first bodies.

By the end of the day, bodies were being unloaded at Juneau. The town's 3000 residents were ill-prepared for such a catastrophe. Earlier in October, torrential rain had flooded most of Juneau's buildings. Moreover, the deadly Spanish flu had begun to rage.

On October 28, the Canadian Pacific Steamship's *Princess Alice* arrived to help, but her crew was quarantined in the harbour. Nevertheless, the *Princess Alice*, originally dispatched to transport survivors, became a "ship of sorrow," taking aboard only bodies. On November 9, the *Alice* departed Juneau, carrying 156 bodies bound for Vancouver and Victoria.

On November 11, at 11 p.m., the *Alice* steamed into Vancouver's Burrard Inlet to berth at Canadian Pacific's Pier D. Her arrival was unheralded, however. The sky on both sides of the inlet blazed with fireworks and roistering crowds that swarmed through the streets. It was Armistice Day, the end of World War I.

Eventually, divers pieced together the fate of the *Sophia*. The force of the storm had lifted and twisted the ship. As she was ripped from her protective "cradle," rocks tore open her hull and the inrush of the sea exploded her boilers. Still, experts estimated, it may have taken an hour for the stricken ship to settle on the bottom of the reef.

Lifeboats would have had no chance in the storm — they would have capsized the instant they touched the water. The sea around the *Sophia* was freezing cold and coated with a suffocating layer of thick, glue-like bunker oil. Survival in the water would have been impossible.

There was, however, one survivor — a dog. Two days after the sinking, the dog, matted with bunker oil and starving, appeared in the hamlet of Auk Bay after swimming 13 kilometres and trudging 7 km from the reef. Within disasters, there are sometimes unexplainable miracles.

Chapter 2
Triumvirate of Tragedy

F or every safe harbour along Canada's shore-lines, the coasts hide a host of hazards, all posing deadly potential for tragedy — none more so than those on the Atlantic Ocean. Three locations in particular have been graveyards for a thousand ships, per-haps more: St. Paul Island in the Cabot Strait, Cape Race on the southern tip of Newfoundland, and Sable Island. These three form the most infamous triumvirate of marine tragedy in Canadian waters.

St. Paul Island and the Wrecks of the *Sovereign* and the *Jessie*
St. Paul Island is worse than inhospitable. Five kilometres long and 1.5 kilometres wide, the island has only two safe landings. Along its shores are ragged, imposing cliffs that are

damp, often ice-coated, and always slippery from constant fog. Only the twisting currents and swirling tides keep the deep, cold, offshore water from freezing. But these are the same currents and tides that also rouse sudden squalls and harsh unpredictable winds, resulting over the years in 350 recorded wrecks on the island — most so shattered on the rocks that no traces remain except for the debris carpeting the ocean floor along the island's entire coastline.

The island's coves and points have acquired names such as Trinity, Aurora, Viceroy, Isabella, Glenroe, and Jessie — all in memory of ships wrecked at these sites. Atlantic Cove is an anomalous name because it does not signify a wreck — it offers one of the few safe landings. Just up the coast from Atlantic Cove is Sovereign Cove. Here, there are 199 graves, the result of the 1814 wreck of the British ship *Sovereign*.

The *Sovereign* was a troop ship carrying a military contingent and officers' families assigned to bolster British wartime efforts against the Americans in the War of 1812. On October 18, having successfully skirted Sable Island and eased past Cape Race, the *Sovereign* encountered St. Paul — eight square kilometres of unyielding rocks. St. Paul absorbed the ship as quickly as a desert absorbs an extra grain of sand.

Thirty-seven people survived the *Sovereign* wreck. They had to wait days on the barren rocks for a lull in the gales that wracked the island. Their rescue was fortunate. As the storms blew themselves out, a fishing boat entered the area. Its crew spotted wreckage and bodies in the water and landed on the narrow beach to investigate. The meagre shoreline was clogged with bodies, left behind by the ebbing tide. There, too, just above the high waterline, huddled the *Sovereign*'s few survivors, many of whom were suffering from severe exposure.

Eventually, labourers had to be recruited from the mainland to scratch out a mass grave for the dead. Only one body was never recovered. Listed in maritime records for the Sovereign Cove area are no less than 15 other shipwrecks.

When the *Jessie* ran up on the rocks of St. Paul during a blizzard on New Year's Day 1825, everyone on board managed to struggle ashore, scaling the ice-encrusted cliffs until they were safe from the crashing waves. Realizing their peril, survivors repeatedly braved the cliffs to salvage what provisions they could from the stricken *Jessie*, which was rapidly breaking up as the storm continued to pound her against the rocks.

Finally, the blizzard abated and survivors were able to build signal fires, which were spotted from Cape North, the tip of mainland Cape Breton. Although only 6.5 kilometres away, Cape North may as well have been on the other side of the Atlantic. The treacherous sea had locked the channel in constantly shifting pack ice that was impossible for a boat to navigate or even for a man to walk across. The survivors could not be helped, nor could they help themselves.

Although they were somewhat sheltered in huts fashioned from scraps of the *Jessie* and other driftwood — probably remnants of other ships — exposure began to take its toll. January passed into February, but the pack ice held. Weakened by exposure and malnutrition, the survivors began to die. February passed into March, and on March 17 or 18, the last survivor of the *Jessie*, Mac Kay, passed away. Kay was a Prince Edward Island merchant and owner of the *Jessie*. He'd recorded the details of the ship's plight in a daily journal. His final entry, written in trembling hand, was on March 17.

In April, sealers salvaged the wreck site. Among the items removed was a distinctive cloak owned by Kay. That fall, Kay's widow encountered a sailor in Charlottetown who was wearing the cloak. Recognizing it from a label she'd embroidered for it herself, and learning the details of its source, she sent a ship to St. Paul to recover the bodies. Only three were found, but among them was her husband — 6.5 impossible kilometres from safety.

Years passed before a lighthouse was erected on St. Paul, and still more passed before a wireless station was built. In 1948, with these improvements, St. Paul proved itself to be a lifesaver rather than a windswept charnel house. That spring, in sleet-thick winds up to 100 kilometres per hour, the sealer *Teazer* was crushed by ice floes. Her entire crew escaped onto the ice and, over 18 hours in the throes of the storm, made their way 32 kilometres across the precarious floes to St. Paul and the safety of its wireless station. A century earlier, they would have been as doomed as the complement of the *Jessie*.

Even today, only the most experienced divers attempt exploration of the wrecks of St. Paul Island.

Cape Race and the Wreck of the *Florizel*

St. Paul Island is the first major hazard facing outbound mariners as they pass beyond the Gulf of St. Lawrence through the Cabot Strait. For inbound sailors, the first landfall they see is Cape Race, at the southern tip of Newfoundland's Avalon Peninsula.

The coastline of Newfoundland, and Cape Race in particular, is fogbound much of the year. Around Cape Race, shifting pack ice and icebergs are common, especially in the spring. The combination of fog, ice, heavy currents, and rocks at Cape Race are a deadly trap for the unwary and the unlucky.

Cape Race took its place in Canadian history in 1904, when the first Marconi radio station was established there to provide wireless communication with ships at sea. At the time the Marconi station was established, according to a St. John's newspaper account, 94 shipwrecks had been recorded at the cape, taking an estimated 2000 lives. Despite the new communications system, the toll continued to rise.

The *Florizel* was a coastal steamer that regularly moved between Newfoundland ports to Halifax and New York. Her captain, William Martin, was considered one of the most knowledgeable and cautious skippers in the coastal service. His ship was equipped with radar and radio and had been built with reinforced bow plates for ice breaking, essential in those waters.

On February 23, 1918, the *Florizel* cast off from St. John's at 8 p.m. with a full cargo and 145 passengers and crew. The barometer was already dropping. At 4:30 a.m. on February 24, a wireless station picked up a distress call. "SOS — *Florizel* ashore near Cape Race. Fast going to pieces."

The ship had been bucking a gale-driven rain. Around midnight, the wind had shifted and the rain had become a blizzard. Compounding that danger, a mechanical failure had rendered the ship powerless. Inevitably, the *Florizel* was driven onto the rocks, immovably skewered through her middle between bow and stern.

By dawn, there were watchers on the cliffs above the cape. Below them in the grey overcast morning was the *Florizel*, still impaled on rocks, only 230 metres from shore.

Thanks to the wireless alert, by noon, three rescue ships were en route, and a medical relief train had been dispatched to the nearest railhead. On shore, impatient, deeply concerned rescue teams waited for the opportunity to cast lines to the *Florizel* so they could begin evacuating survivors to land.

By this time, only the ship's bow and forecastle were above water. The sea was running heavy. Waves crashed relentlessly over the vessel, slowly shredding her strength. Unless the sea calmed, the ship's break-up was imminent and rescue of the survivors would be impossible. Everyone present conceded that the ship herself was lost.

During the afternoon, seven bodies washed ashore. Still, potential rescuers had hope. Periodically, people could be seen waving from the *Florizel*. After dark, tiny lights flickered, went out, then flickered again.

Finally, early the next morning, the sea relented. Nearby, the three rescue ships managed to get close enough to launch dories. Three were almost immediately capsized — though the sea was easing off, it was by no means finished. Nonetheless, rescuers persisted.

The first dory to reach the *Florizel* was from the steamer *Gordon C.* Her captain, a man named Perry, and a crewman made several trips to the wrecked vessel, rescuing 20 passengers before their dory capsized and they required rescue themselves. Both men were severely injured. A boat from another ship, HMS *Terra Nova*, also capsized, drowning a young Royal Navy reservist before he could be saved. One passenger named Sullivan, a 198-pound man wearing a heavy cloth overcoat, fell into the sea as he was being rescued. He had to be towed 70 metres while clinging to a rope before his rescuers dared try to get him into a dory without capsizing it.

By 8 o'clock that evening, 44 people had been rescued. During the efforts, one rescuer had drowned, bringing the final death toll to 94 passengers. All suffered from exposure due to the frigid temperatures and constant dampness. But many were likely spared thanks to the cool heads that prevailed on board. Despite the knowledge that many lives had been lost in the early minutes after the ship ran aground, aboard the *Florizel* there was neither panic nor chaos throughout the ordeal.

William Martin was the last person to leave the ship, a

captain to the end. Within days, all trace of the *Florizel* was gone and the sea seethed as before, preparing for the next storm, and the next ship.

Small Mercies on Sable Island

Unlike at St. Paul and Cape Race, Sable Island has no razor-edged rocks lining the shore or hiding just offshore below the water's surface. Rather, it is a monstrous sand bar — a low, slender, crescent-shaped island about 40 kilometres long.

Sable's real menace lies just under the water on each side of the island, where other sand bars run like multiple, uneven corrugations. The bars have a singular quality: they constantly move in the converging currents of the warm Gulf Stream and the frigid Labrador Current. This convergence also swathes Sable Island in dense fog most of the year and slashes the sea around it with sudden storms.

Sable Island tastes almost every storm that comes up the Atlantic coast of North America and many storms that swoop down from the eastern Arctic. The island hangs like a pirate's cutlass, always poised to slice another luckless ship into flotsam with a casual swipe of a sharp, hard-edged 12-metre wave.

Since the first recorded wreck in 1583, more than 350 have followed. In fog and storm, ships have run aground onto the bars, then been pounded to driftwood by waves made fiercer by the shallows.

The worst disasters occurred prior to the 20th century,

during the years of sails and wooden ships. Navigation in those days was often by dead reckoning and very much at the mercy of prevailing winds. Ships trapped on sandbars could only hope that a shifting wind would back them off the sand.

In 1746, an armada of 71 French warships bent on creating havoc along the Nova Scotia and New England coastlines fell afoul of Sable's shores. Already decimated by scurvy and an outbreak of typhus, the crews and troops were ill prepared for their encounter. At least four ships were lost outright to the island. Those that escaped were so damaged that only half the armada made it back to France. As many as 300 men from the four ships may have lost their lives.

In the 1800s, rescue stations and lighthouses were built on the island, both of which saved scores of ships and hundreds of lives. An unlikely visitor in 1853 also indirectly saved the lives of many. Dorothea Dix was a famous philanthropist and social reformer from Boston. At the time, she was in the Maritimes lobbying for improved treatment of mentally ill people. Her visit to Sable Island was a side trip. She arrived on a Tuesday and on Thursday witnessed the rescue of the crew of a grounded schooner, the *Guide*.

Thoroughly impressed by the efforts of the rescuers, Dix realized just how much better they could do with modern equipment. Upon her return to Boston, she set about raising money to purchase the best equipment available.

The new equipment arrived on November 11, 1854 — four lifeboats, a mortar device to fire lines from the shore to grounded ships, and an enclosed life capsule that could be pulled between ship and shore in the roughest seas. On November 27, the equipment was put to use when the *Arcadia*, carrying 168 passengers and crew, went aground in a gale. The largest of the new lifeboats made six trips at the height of the storm, taking 80 people off the ship. By noon the next day, everyone had been rescued, as well as much of their belongings and the ship's cargo. Without the new equipment, all would have been lost.

Dorothea Dix came to be known as "the Angel of Sable Island." The work of people such as Dix has saved many lives there — one of the small mercies that has helped to mitigate the latent tragedy lurking under the water for the unwary and unfortunate.

Chapter 3
Human Factors

n sea and land, and in the air, the unpredictable forces of nature have long been the cause of terrible disasters. Prevention of such disasters is quite often impossible, though calamitous results can sometimes be reduced by heeding early warning signs, or with prompt emergency responses.

Other disasters have different characteristics. These are disasters that people bring upon themselves or, as has been more likely, bring upon other people. Financial greed, complacency, ambition, neglect, ignorance, error, oversight — these are a few of the human causes of major Canadian disasters.

The Shore Too Far
On a sunny June afternoon in 1857, the decks of the paddle

steamer *Montreal* were jammed. Back then, the steamer business was fiercely competitive. Fares were reduced and steamers often set off overcrowded. Moreover, to cut costs, safety features were sometimes sacrificed.

Including passengers and crew, there were 400 people aboard the 76-metre vessel. All were emigrants from Scotland on their way to Montreal, and more than half planned to become new Canadians. As they looked from the crowded decks across the broad St. Lawrence River, they were likely happy that the longest part of their arduous journey was over. Down in the engine room, stokers vigorously shoveled coal to bring the boilers to full steam.

About 15 kilometres outside Quebec City, the *Montreal* caught fire. The fire originated in the boiler room, where highly flammable wood panelling was ignited due to its close proximity to the almost red-hot boilers. In inland steamers of the day, wood panelling was preferred over steel because it was cheaper and lighter, enabling the steamers to travel faster and also to travel in shallower water. However, the wood proved to be somewhat of a hazard — this was the third time in as many months that the *Montreal*'s panelling had ignited.

As the fire raged through the *Montreal*, the ship's two lifeboats — her only lifeboats — were launched. Overloaded, both boats immediately capsized, dumping occupants into the river. At the time, the ice was barely off the St. Lawrence, and the river's currents were running fast and cold. Undoubtedly sensing disaster, the captain headed for shore at full speed. Beaching the ship would have allowed many to make land, but 240 metres from shore, the *Montreal* ran aground on a rock. Thus impaled, the wooden vessel rapidly burned to the waterline.

Another Montreal-bound steamer, the *Napoleon*, was nearby and managed to rescue 59 passengers from the river. More were rescued by the crew of a boat being towed by the *Napoleon*. Within 20 minutes — the time it took for the *Napoleon* to turn about, reach the scene, and begin picking up survivors — 200 people had drowned, many of them children. Many others were women, weighed down by the cumbersome dress and layered clothing of the time.

Margaret Bloomfield of Edinburgh, mother of four, lost two of her children. She had waited for years while her husband worked as a Grand Trunk Railway engineer to save money for his family's passage to North America. That day, she saved herself by leaping from the burning ship, then clinging to a rope until she was rescued. All the while, she clutched one child in her arms and another in her mouth, the latter so fiercely that she lost two teeth. Days later, Margaret and her two surviving children were reunited with her husband and together the mourning family completed their journey to Montreal, by rail.

The final death toll of the tragedy was based on the number of recovered bodies. Because many tickets were sold on the docks in the last minutes before departure, passenger lists were incomplete. The normal practice was to complete the lists during disembarkation. Many victims may have been swept by the fearsome current into the anonymous clutches of the North Atlantic Ocean.

In the aftermath of the *Montreal* tragedy, steamer competition declined, more safety measures were implemented, and the shipowners exercised more caution. However, as long as wooden steamers plied the rivers and lakes of Canada, steamer fires were commonplace, and, as a result, many hundreds of people — passengers and crew — died.

The *Montreal* disaster was the worst of its kind, not only because of the appalling loss of life, but because it combined among its causes greed, neglect, and oversight — most by people who may never have set foot on the steamer's decks. This was a dooming recipe for 200 innocent souls. No culpability was ever assigned and no one was ever prosecuted.

The *Noronic*: Toronto's Blazing Night to Remember
The *Noronic* was the doyenne of the Great Lakes. In 1949, still sleek and regal at 36 years of age, she was a veteran of Great Lakes excursions. One brochure described a trip on the *Noronic* as "the ideal route from east to west." Another invited people to come aboard for a "delightful cruise vacation."

Unfortunately, the *Noronic* wore a heavy flammable robe. So polished had she been over the years that her woodwork gleamed, thick with layers of lemon oil. The floors of the ship's cabins, salons, and dining rooms reflected every image in innumerable coats of varnish. Her ironworks, including the outside decking and railings, had been painted every spring before the summer cruise season began — one coat for each of her 36 years.

On September 14, 1949, the *Noronic* embarked on her last pleasure cruise of that season, a seven-day excursion that started from Detroit. It was to be seven days of pampered travel through the picturesque Thousand Islands with a stop in Toronto for a night on the town before returning to Detroit. The ship's pace was leisurely and the weather was perfect.

With 524 passengers and 171 crew aboard, the *Noronic* moored in Toronto on September 16. As this was the final cruise of the season and the last night out for all, Captain William Taylor granted shore leave to all but 15 crew members. Even Captain Taylor himself was drawn into the city for a few hours to dine with friends.

By 2:30 a.m., most passengers had returned to the ship and were in bed. However, Don Church, a fire insurance inspector on holiday from Ohio, wasn't. He discovered what appeared to be a minor fire in a corridor closet. With the help of Garth O'Neill, a ship's bellboy, Church attempted to put out the burning linens with hand extinguishers. These were insufficient. The two men soon found an emergency fire hose, but the hose was dry. There was no water pressure.

The fire escaped into the corridor. Fuelled by the oil-saturated woodwork, it quickly spread from deck to deck. Corridors and cabins were soon choked with smoke, signalling that flames were close behind.

From the wharf, two watchmen on patrol noticed smoke wisping from the great ship. They immediately phoned in the alarm, but by the time the first firefighters arrived, just minutes later, the *Noronic* was fully engulfed, flames bounding 30 metres into the air. "The ship went up like a paint factory," said one severely burned passenger.

Ross Leitch operated a small water taxi in the Toronto harbour. He was about to berth his boat for the night when he heard the sirens. Casting his lines, he quickly made his way to the scene. In the fire's eerie glow, he could see heads bobbing in the water. In jumping, one passenger crashed through the taxi's cabin roof. Another landed on its forward deck. Some passengers also escaped down the aerial ladders firefighters stretched from the dock. One photograph shows a dapper passenger in suit and tie descending a ladder. He's smoking a cigar and carrying a small valise.

By 5 a.m., two and a half hours after the first alarm, the fire department had the blaze under control. In that brief time, they had poured 6.5 million litres of water onto the ship. The *Noronic* was now a smouldering hulk, settled on the harbour bottom. Over her hung a grey reeking pall of smoke.

Throughout the day, rescuers scoured the harbour and sifted the still-cooling wreckage for bodies. On board they found no survivors — the fire had burned so hot that, in some cases, even bone had been incinerated. The final toll was 118 dead, 14 of whom were unidentifiable. All were passengers. To the credit of Ross Leitch and his crew, as well as Cyril Cole and Robert Anderson, two police officers who had dived into the water to hold survivors until Leitch could reach them, only one of those deaths was a result of drowning. While the fire's origin was confirmed to be in a linen closet, the exact cause remained unknown. An appointed commission concluded, however, that the *Noronic*'s owners and captain had failed to provide adequate fire detection patrols and training in firefighting for the crew, and that they'd had no emergency evacuation plan. The owners' response was to reprimand Captain Taylor and suspend him from service for one year. Shattered in spirit, Captain Taylor, though legally exonerated, took early retirement and spent the balance of his working life as a hotel desk clerk in Sarnia.

Ocean Danger

At 30 storeys high, the semi-submersible oil rig Ocean Ranger was the largest in the Hibernia oil field, off the coast of Newfoundland. Indeed, it was the largest in the world. It was thought to be impervious to the worst storms and ice threats the North Atlantic could hurl at it. Like the *Titanic*, the Ocean Ranger had proudly been declared unsinkable.

On February 6, 1982, the Ocean Ranger suddenly developed a 10- to 15-degree list. The 90 men working aboard were ordered over the PA system to assemble at lifeboat stations. Here they waited in the cold for a PA announcement to board lifeboats and abandon ship. (In truth, it was remarkable that so many workers had obediently assembled at the lifeboat stations. Usually the workers ignored messages on the PA system. In fact, on other occasions, workers had gone so far as to stuff the PA speakers with rags because they blared incessantly day and night.)

Although the actual order to board the lifeboats was not given, mayhem ensued. Gordon Noseworthy was working on the rig that day, and he managed to position himself to board a boat. "The lifeboat handles about 58 people on board," he later said, "and she must have had 65. Some fellows at the lifeboat station during the list … didn't wear their life jackets. I remember one fellow just had a tee shirt on and he was freezing. I was scared to death that day. I was frozen solid. Didn't know what to do. We never had the training for that."

The cause of the list was discovered and corrected, and the men were ordered back to work. Soon, the business of drilling for oil resumed. The personnel on the *Ocean Ranger* had dodged a bullet. The massive rig remained "unsinkable."

In keeping with U.S. Coast Guard regulations (under which the rig operated because it was American-owned), practice emergency drills were periodically carried out. The lack of a controlled, organized response to the list on February 6 — more serious than a mock drill — was described as typical.

Then, on Valentine's Day, a winter storm tore across the North Atlantic. Blizzard conditions, freezing temperatures, winds of 168 kilometres per hour, and 5-storey waves battered the Ocean Ranger. Throughout much of that day, the rig withstood the storm's onslaught.

At 10 p.m., Jack Jacobsen, the rig boss, radioed to shore that the Ocean Ranger was fine. Three hours later, however, he sent a message advising that the rig was listing and in trouble. Shortly after, his radio operator, Rick Flynn, sent a mayday call asking for mobilization of search and rescue operations from the mainland. Finally, at 1:30 a.m., Flynn radioed that the order to abandon the rig had gone out to personnel.

Unabated, the storm continued. Helicopter search and rescue crews scrambled to get to bases onshore. Many rescue crew members had to be transported by four-wheel-drive vehicles to the airstrips due to the blizzard's ferocity — the same storm that was pummelling the Ocean Ranger. Meanwhile, the closest vessel to the Ocean Ranger was the *Seaforth Highlander*, a rig supply ship. According to Ralph Jorgenson, the *Seaforth*'s first mate, the ship's crew immediately spotted a lifeboat only two metres away, with one survivor visible. As the *Seaforth*'s crew cast a line to the survivor, they saw other men gathering at the one side of the lifeboat. Unfortunately, the weight of the men, combined with heavy seas, capsized the boat, pitching them into the frigid water. Hypothermia and shock immobilized the men almost instantly. They were unable to help themselves, not even to cling to the overturned lifeboat. They disappeared into the storm while the crewmen on the *Seaforth* watched helplessly, the sea running far too high for them to launch a rescue dory. All 84 men aboard the Ocean Ranger perished in the disaster.

The Ocean Ranger carried sufficient lifeboats for all workers on board. Two were "enclosed survival systems," watertight cocoons capable of holding 58 people each. When rescuers eventually pulled these lifeboats from the ocean, both were severely damaged and empty. The remaining lifeboats were also recovered. They, too, were damaged — probably, experts speculated, when launched from the rig.

Employer logs, confirmed by worker testimony, showed that training for the launching of lifeboats had never been undertaken in rough seas. The only launch drills had been from the protected St. John's Harbour sea wall, and these were undertaken by only 40 of the 200 employees who rotated work on the rig.

A final, far more significant finding was made by the Royal Commission inquiry into the Ocean Ranger disaster. Had the ballast control operator been properly trained, the commission concluded, the need to abandon the rig and subsequent tragedy could have been prevented. The fierce storm that had begun on February 14 had sent a wave washing into an open porthole in the Ocean Ranger's ballast control room, short-circuiting the equipment and causing a list. A short time later, the ballast control operator had made a fatal error. Instead of emptying the ballast tank on the side where the rig was listing, he pumped in more water, increasing the list and ultimately sinking the rig.

Frank Jennings provided the commission with the most telling testimony. Jennings, who had been a ballast control officer on the Ocean Ranger between 1976 and 1981, testified that when he was hired, he received no formal training. He didn't even know what the job entailed. On his first day on the rig, when he walked into the ballast control room, the solitary operator simply got up and left, leaving Jennings to figure out the meters, computers, and other devices for himself. If he ran into a problem, Jennings said, he hoped "someone would come along who could help."

After February, the disaster moved into courtrooms, corporate offices, and conference rooms. Poignantly, however, in July, two life vests from the Ocean Ranger were recovered by fishermen near the Faroe Islands, off the north coast of Scotland — the Atlantic has a way of passing along warning to others on the water. No other offshore rig has sunk since the Ocean Ranger.

Spanning the Waters: High Steel Disasters

Oceans, lakes, and rivers always present a challenge. For most people, the challenge is how to navigate them. For a few, the bridge builders, the challenge is how to span them.

The Mohawk men of the Caughnewaga (today called Kahnewake) Indian Reserve, located 10 kilometres southwest of Montreal, knew how to build bridges. At the turn of the 20th century, they began stringing girders for bridges and skyscrapers throughout North America and were soon ranked among the finest high steelworkers in the world.

Their skills were first recognized in 1886, when Mohawk crews worked on the construction of a railway bridge over the St. Lawrence River. They had insisted on getting jobs on the project because part of the bridge was on reserve land.

The Mohawk would eventually go on to work on such projects as the Empire State Building, the Chrysler Building, and the World Trade Center. They would pound rivets on the Triborough, Verranzano, George Washington, and Golden Gate Bridges. They would also work on what was to become the longest cantilever bridge in the world — the Quebec Bridge, which spans the St. Lawrence River at Quebec City.

For years, the Quebec Bridge did not get off the drawing board due to lack of money. Finally, in 1903, the federal government guaranteed financing. The chief engineer of the project was Theodore Cooper, considered one of the best bridge designers in North America. Cooper suggested that the cantilever section extend 548 metres of the total bridge length of 1006 metres. This would significantly reduce costs because the support piers could be built on dry land rather than in the water, where cofferdams would have to be constructed while the work was carried out. Work commenced, and by the summer of 1907, the bridge was close to completion.

The critical piece was the suspended centre span, the final link between the two shores. Work on it began in July.

Almost immediately, stress problems were noticed. The farther the span reached out over the river, the more severe the problems became. Cooper, based in New York, was informed of the problems and provided advice, but his authority was distant and no one on-site could do more than make suggestions. Moreover, Cooper was distracted by ill health, making travel for onsite inspections prohibitive for him.

On August 29, at approximately 11:30 a.m., matters became so critical that Cooper asked Norman McLure, his on-site inspecting engineer (who happened to be in New York at the time), to send a wire to the site ordering that no additional load be placed on the span. Cooper's message was explicit: "Add no more load to bridge until after due consideration of facts. McLure will be over at 5 o'clock." The message would have immediately shut down most of the work.

In his haste to get back to the site, however, McLure failed to send the message, and work continued into the afternoon. At about 3:15 p.m., Cooper sent the same message as a backup, but on-site construction supervisors decided at 5:15 to ignore the note and continue work. The smallest of the traveller cranes, which carried and positioned materials for the high steelworkers, moved onto the span.

Although only a riveter, Alexandre Beauvais could recognize a problem on the high steel. He had already noticed that some support beams were uncharacteristically bent. During the afternoon, while checking his morning's work, he observed that several rivets had popped, indicating a strain they couldn't counter. Near shift's end, just as he brought the matter to his foreman's attention and was assured it didn't matter — "they were no worse than others," he was told — the south end of the bridge, with an ear-shattering, drawn-out shriek, collapsed onto the riverbank and into the river.

Although injured, Beauvais survived. Seventy-five other workers did not. Of these, 33 were from the Caughnewaga Reserve, killed in a tragedy that reached into every family of the close-knit community. Angus Montour died trapped in nearly 40,000 tons of twisted steel. His brother, Thomas, survived by jumping 25 metres into the river and swimming to shore. John Montour, also related, survived, too. Only minutes earlier, he had been sent off the bridge to buy food for the crew.

The most miraculous escape was that of the traveller crane operator. As the bridge and traveller crane began to fall, he jumped out the window. As he fell, he followed the crane and girders down into the seething river, escaping with only bruises.

Shortly after the disastrous collapse, work resumed on the bridge. Cooper and his team of structural engineers were able to piece together the causes of the initial collapse — primarily miscalculations in material tolerances — and to rectify them. Due to steel shortages, work was sporadic, but finally, on September 11, 1916, the centre span was set to be raised, marking a masterful engineering feat. Just as the raised span was being slotted into place, a hydraulic jack malfunctioned, causing the span to twist, then crash into the river, taking 13 more steelworkers to their deaths. Undeterred, the builders worked on, completing the bridge in 1917.

Technology has greatly changed the discipline of engineering today. Tolerances can be precisely measured, and data from bridge-building work from all over the world is readily available to designers. Canadian structural engineers also have an emotional reminder "to measure and calculate, then measure again" — an iron ring that is presented upon graduation as a reminder of the Quebec Bridge disaster.

Chapter 4
Risk Rides Steel Wheels

hroughout the latter half of the 19th century, railroad building from town to town, city to city, and coast to coast inexorably led to the decline in use of inland waterways for transportation.

In the 20th century, rail was then applied for mass transportation inside cities, notably streetcars and, later, subways. Development moved fast, for vast fortunes were to be made from the new mode. As happened with the advent of steamships, safety measures did not keep apace, and the few measures that were put in place by regulation were sometimes circumvented in the name of cost or efficiency.

The Desjardins Canal Train Wreck
The sound of steel wheels clicking over the rails was likely as

comforting to Samuel Zimmerman as the rustle of bills and rattle of coins in his Niagara Falls bank. A well-known railway man, Zimmerman had started out as a contractor helping to dig the Welland Canal and had then moved on to extend the Great Western Railway to Niagara Falls and points south with a bridge across to the American side. In 1857, he lived in Niagara Falls, where he was building a palatial home for his family.

On March 12, along with 100 other passengers, he boarded the Great Western train in Toronto, destined for Niagara Falls. The trip was his chance to relax after a day of serious business dealings. It would also be fast. Zimmerman had seen to that, having successfully lobbied against the rail regulation that all trains must fully stop before a swing bridge and proceed at reduced speed across its length.

The train westbound from Toronto was short. Along with the engine — the 23-ton Oxford — it had only two passenger cars and a baggage car.

Just outside Hamilton, the train proceeded across the wooden swing bridge over the frozen Desjardins Canal at about 11 kilometres per hour, a good speed for trains of the day. Recounting the events of the night, some local residents remembered that the bridge was in disrepair. They said that although the bridge was only three years old, its supporting timbers were rotten, and the bridge was shaky at best. Speculations notwithstanding, what is known absolutely is that as the train crossed the bridge, it left the bridge track and plummeted 20 metres into the partially frozen canal.

Engineer Alexander Burnfield must have sensed a problem as soon as the Oxford was on the bridge because he immediately whistled to brake the train. Michael Duffy, his brakeman, peered from his position at the rear of the baggage car. Ahead, according to his later testimony, he saw the bridge timbers snapping beneath the engine. There was no time to brake. Instead, Duffy jumped from the train.

The engine's weight and momentum were enough to shatter the metre-thick ice coating the canal. Burnfield was thrown clear, but broke his neck when he hit the ice. Missing the water, the baggage car ruptured on the canal's shore. The lead passenger car somersaulted in the air and crashed flat on its roof into a miasma of ice shards, freezing water, bridge timbers, and engine wreckage, instantly killing most of its riders.

Owen Doyle, a passenger in the first car, managed to free himself from the wreckage. His niece survived because a passenger pushed her clear as the car settled into the canal. His nephew was also saved, rescued by a woman named Mrs. House, who saw the mishap from her home and was able to reach him as he desperately clung on to a window frame.

The second passenger car landed on its end, jutting out of the canal as prominently as a tall tombstone in a cemetery. For those in this car, the event must have seemed as though it was occurring in slow motion. The train conductor and at least two passengers were able to leap from the car before it went over the edge. Although 10 passengers in the second car died, many escaped with injuries because the force of the crash was absorbed by the thickly cushioned double-facing seats.

Rescuers quickly arrived from Hamilton. Battling the cold and darkness, the steep, slippery incline into the canal, and shifting wreckage, they managed to free the survivors, 18 of whom were seriously injured. They also recovered the bodies of 59 people, including Samuel Zimmerman.

The inquest blamed a broken axle on the engine for the derailment but never addressed the deeper questions, such as what broke the axle or whether the break would have been detected had the train stopped before proceeding onto the bridge. The Oxford had recently undergone an extensive overhaul in Great Western's Hamilton engine maintenance shop. This was its first trip since.

No one questioned the condition of the bridge, perhaps not wishing to risk a lawsuit. Notwithstanding the considerable wealth and political influence of the Great Western to bring counter-suit, the Town of Dundas, which had built the bridge for 25 percent less than the government had provided it (perhaps cutting some corners in the process) would doubtless have also moved authoritatively to stifle any allegations.

There was one lingering result. Trains in the area began to stop before venturing onto a bridge span, and for a brief time, many passengers would get off, walk across the bridge, and reboard the train on the other side.

Several years after the disaster, a proposal was put forward to build a new bridge, but with the accident still fresh in the minds of local people, the public mounted an outcry that stopped the project.

The St. Hilaire Train Wreck

Today, regulations for the operation of trains fill volumes. During rail's early years, however, there were few regulations. One standout was that trains had to come to a full stop at swing bridges. As the Desjardins Canal disaster indicated, exemptions were sometimes obtained, most often to speed passenger service.

Seven years after the Desjardins mishap, another railroad swing bridge figured prominently in a major Canadian disaster, this time at St. Hilaire, Quebec.

At the time, the trains on the Grand Trunk Railway along the shores of the St. Lawrence River were often overloaded with immigrants heading from Quebec City to Montreal. Business was so brisk that freight and grain cars were fitted with benches to carry excess passengers.

One such train pulled out of Quebec City late in the afternoon of June 29, 1864. Jammed onto the train were an estimated 467 immigrants who had just arrived from Eastern Europe. (Passenger lists for these immigrant trains were often inaccurate, resulting in estimated rather than actual numbers.) At the throttle was William Burney, an engineer with just 11 days' experience, no training, and no knowledge of the track that lay ahead. With 11 cars, all windowless, this was an exceptionally long train for the period.

On the rail route to Montreal, the track takes a hard right
turn, then immediately descends to a steel swing bridge over
the Richelieu River near the town of St. Hilaire. The descent
is steep enough that an engineer must begin braking as the
train comes out of the curve if it is to be stopped before moving onto the bridge. Unfamiliar with the route, Burney didn't
begin braking.

The speeding train might have rattled across the bridge
without incident, a matter then of simply having broken a
regulation. But, at the same time, a string of loaded barges
was passing underneath and the bridge was open. Burney's
"Immigrant Special" was about to become Canada's worst
rail disaster.

Propelled by its own bulk and the string of loaded cars,
the engine soared off the bridge, hung briefly in space, then
crashed down onto a barge in the river, dragging the cars
with it. Burney had applied the emergency brake when he
saw potential catastrophe, but he was far too late. Car after
car crashed down on top of one another, wooden freight cars
instantly crushed to kindling.

Burney survived the crash, although two other crew
members did not. Hardly anyone escaped uninjured.
Throughout the night, desperate rescuers performed surgery
in a shack by the riverbank. A second train, fitted as a hospital, arrived in the morning to transport victims to Montreal.
In all, 97 passengers and two train crew members died.

William Burney was subsequently pilloried by the

public and the court. He did not testify at his negligence trial. Nor did he have a lawyer. In the heat of the moment, Burney was found guilty and sentenced to 10 years in prison, a sentence that was reduced after an appeal. The railway administration was found to be faultless, despite having failed to provide training for its novice engineer.

The Point Ellice Bridge Tram Wreck

A streetcar, the most mundane of public transportation vehicles, would seem an unlikely prospect for disaster. However, in May 1896, in Victoria, British Columbia, one streetcar proved otherwise.

Then, as today, the Victoria Day weekend was a time for excursions, gala outdoor events, and fireworks. Nowhere in Canada in 1896 were these festivities more elaborate than in the queen's namesake city of Victoria.

On May 26, as part of celebrations, a mock sea battle was to be enacted at the nearby Esquimault Naval Base, a leisurely ride by electric streetcar from the city centre. The event would be a highlight of the holiday. Huge crowds were expected.

Every streetcar heading for the naval base was crowded. By the time the No. 16 streetcar reached the Point Ellice Bridge en route to the base, it was carrying 140 passengers — its capacity was 34. The streetcar was so overflowing that many passengers were riding on the platform or clinging precariously to the car's narrow sideboards. No one seemed to care though — everyone on board was in a party mood.

Traversing an inlet, the Point Ellice Bridge was made from a combination of steel and wood. Beginning in 1885, the bridge had served streetcar and horse-drawn traffic, but by 1896 it was beginning to show signs of wear. In 1893, it had suddenly sagged a full metre under the weight of a streetcar. Repairs were hastily carried out, but those driving any conveyances over the bridge were advised to go slow, lest the old span be shaken from its pylons.

Whatever speed car No. 16 was travelling at didn't matter. What mattered was the bridge. The weight of the overcrowded streetcar was simply too much. As No. 16 rattled onto the centre span, the span gave out, pieces of it splashing into the water seconds before the streetcar.

The passengers riding the platforms and sideboards were the luckiest. Most were thrown clear as No. 16 tumbled toward the water. Of those who managed to hang on, several were injured and others were trapped beneath the car.

The streetcar hit the water on its side and immediately sank. People on the upside of the sinking car managed to scramble or swim out open windows. Those on the underside were not so fortunate. The streetcar became their tomb.

William Scott was one of the lucky ones. He'd been riding a sideboard and was thrown clear. The young man then dove down several times to the wreck to pull people free, saving four lives. The record of Scott's heroism is preserved in the archives of the local daily newspaper, where he was employed at the time.

The final death toll was 55. Onlookers and rescuers predicted it would have been much higher except a regatta was happening at the time. Holidayers in this armada of sailboats, canoes, and rowboats immediately began hauling survivors from the water. Fortunately, the inlet was not very wide, so survivors who could swim and were uninjured were able to reach shore.

To date, the collapse of the Point Ellice Bridge is Victoria's worst disaster and North America's worst streetcar accident.

Shortcut to Disaster: The Rogers Pass Avalanche

The distance between Revelstoke and Golden in British Columbia is relatively short. Yet, when a road was finally put through (officially opened in 1940), it was called the Big Bend because it looped nearly 320 kilometres to avoid the more obvious route through Rogers Pass — the most avalanche-prone area in the Rocky Mountains. Built mostly for logging trucks, the Big Bend comprised hairpin turns, log bridges, and tree and rock falls around every curve. Nevertheless, it was considered safer than Rogers Pass and, for road builders, an easier route to build.

Railway construction in the late 1800s, however, was on a tighter budget, and the line did not follow a round-about route. Instead, it was pushed over Rogers Pass, a much shorter distance than Big Bend, but also riskier. Over sections of track considered to be the most vulnerable, sturdy snow sheds were built to divert the avalanches.

Section foreman John Anderson knew every rail and tie in the Rogers Pass. He knew where avalanches would bury the track in winter and where mud slides and washouts would tear out the track in spring and fall. His job was to keep the track open. When that failed, his job was to get it reopened, preferably before the next scheduled train had to get through.

Each winter since the route had opened in 1886, avalanches regularly closed the pass, but in 1910, the railway was prepared. Anderson had scores of men on call and 110-ton rotary ploughs at the ready. The rotary ploughs were specially designed to clear rail lines. They could churn through heavily packed snow and throw it beyond the rail bed, even adjusting for rail lines where one side was a vertical cliff and the other a precipice.

As it turned out, 1910 was a particularly bad year for avalanches. There were many delays as track was cleared of snow and debris, and even further delays as new track was laid. The force of an avalanche could tear out roadbeds and rails, hurling them thousands of metres down sheer mountainsides.

On March 4, the heavy snows on Cheops Mountain, overlooking the track on the Revelstoke end of the pass, broke loose. If the avalanche had occurred minutes earlier, a passenger train would have been buried. Indeed, the vibrations from the passing train may have triggered the avalanche.

Soon, Anderson and a work crew were on the scene with a massive rotary plough and a locomotive. Together, they began carving a canyon through the snow and debris, clearing the track sufficiently for trains to pass, with seven-metre walls of snow on each side. When the plough became clogged, the men moved forward to remove debris.

The work was going well. Anderson took the opportunity to trudge out to inform Revelstoke division headquarters that the track would be clear in two hours. He left 63 men hard at work. When he returned, he found one man, barely alive.

A second avalanche had roared down the mountain from the opposite side. The 165-ton work locomotive had been flipped by the force, and the plough had been lifted out of the trough and hurled like a frail jack pine seedling. The trough had disappeared. So, too, had 62 men.

In their frantic search for survivors, more than 600 people — miners, trappers, lumberjacks, and townsfolk — laboured in a blizzard throughout the entire next day. All they found was evidence of the avalanche's speed. Many victims were found standing. Within the cut, beside the track, was a man transfixed, rolling a cigarette. Another still held his pick over his head. Three men stood together, perhaps conferring. One held his pipe. They were frozen in place, like the victims of ancient Pompeii.

By 1911, 25 years since the route had opened, the avalanches at Rogers Pass had claimed more than 200 lives. As a result, the general public demanded safer railroads. By then, the railway had also conceded that the avalanches (and spring washouts in the same area) had beaten them.

Canadian Pacific successfully undertook the largest engineering project in the history of British Columbia, other than building the railway itself. The company carved the famous Connaught Tunnel through a mountain to bypass the worst areas. Wide enough to accommodate double track, the tunnel extends eight kilometres and is still in use today.

The number of avalanches in the Rogers Pass area has not diminished since 1910. Each year, they continue to roar down the mountainsides, still claiming lives. Now, however, almost all the people in the mountains are there for recreational purposes, such as skiing and snowmobiling. Despite a continuing increase in the number of recreational users, on average the number of fatalities has dropped, primarily because of better understanding of avalanche causes and use of sophisticated early warning and prevention systems.

Today, most of the Big Bend is closed, but paralleling the rail line over Rogers Pass is the TransCanada Highway. Since the highway opened, not a single car or truck has been swept away by an avalanche.

The Hinton Train Wreck

Riding a train through the prairies can be hypnotic. The grades and curves are few, the speed is constant, and the landscape is unbroken, especially in February, when all there is to see from the windows of the skydome car are stubble fields and dirt-smeared patches of melting snow.

On February 8, 1986, for the passengers and crew on

Via Rail's No. 4 train heading east, the hypnotic effect would not yet have kicked in. The train had just come down from the high country. Although the land was rapidly flattening into a featureless expanse, the view east of Hinton, Alberta, still offered a few lakes and forests. At 8:40 a.m., some passengers were still sleeping. Others, wakeful, had their minds on breakfast and the view from the train.

Transcontinental Via No. 4 consisted of three diesel engines, two steam-generating units, and nine passenger cars. It was travelling on a single track. As is customary, it had the right of way, which meant any oncoming train was obliged to slow or stop as necessary to let it pass.

Well-coordinated signal lights at intervals along the tracks usually ensured a flawless process, requiring only that engineers alertly follow instructions. The signal lights were operated by central traffic control systems that had been in place across the country for two years. In traffic control centres, system operators could determine the location of any train at any time. There was also an override that prevented a dispatcher from accidentally ordering two trains onto a single track at the same time. The system was state of the art.

Heading west that morning was a CN freight train made up of 114 cars, mostly laden with prairie grain bound for the massive grain carriers riding anchor in Vancouver's harbour. Along with these were several freight cars carrying bulk sulphur and flatcars loaded with steel pipe. The freight train clipped along at 40 kilometres per hour on a double track that ran out 18 kilometres east of Hinton.

For reasons that have not been determined, the freight train ran a yellow-over-red signal 13 kilometres from where the double track ended, a warning to slow down and prepare to stop. Then, 42 kilometres later, the freight sped through a triple red signal, the order to stop. Now it was too late. The freight train moved onto the single track, still travelling at 40 kilometres per hour. Just 70 metres farther, it slammed head-on into Via No. 4.

The two trains collided with a combined force of more than 11 million kilograms. Seventy-six freight cars derailed and scattered like matchsticks, spewing thousands of tons of grain along the track — in some places three metres deep. The freight train engineer and trainman, J. Hudson and M. Edwards respectively, were in the lead locomotive. They were killed instantly. The train's conductor, Wayne Smith, who rode in the caboose more than a kilometre behind, survived uninjured.

The horror of the disaster was in Via No. 4's passenger cars. The lead passenger car was destroyed beyond recognition, partly due to a fire that raged through the wreckage as a result of diesel fuel spilled from ruptured tanks.

An unidentified, severely injured passenger from the lead passenger car described the first moments of the collision. Thrown from his seat, which had been torn from its anchor bolts, the man was engulfed in a massive fireball. He was then buried under a torrent of grain that, luckily, smothered the fire. Digging his way out, the man managed to crawl from the crumpled wreckage.

Rescue workers, many of them derailment and train collision specialists, needed two days to get into the first car. There they found the remains of 17 passengers. Five more from other cars also died. Along with 4 crewmen, this brought the final number of dead to 23.

An intensive investigation could not determine the cause of the disaster. The central control system was found to be operating properly. In the freight train cab, investigators found the standard "dead man's pedal," a foot pedal the engineer had to keep depressed at all times. If the engineer relaxed, the brakes would automatically activate, but it was sometimes the custom among engineers to weight the pedal for their own comfort's sake. The trainman, also in the cab, had an emergency button within easy reach that would have triggered the brakes. Finally, 114 cars behind, was the conductor, connected by radio to the cab. He, too, had an emergency brake button. All three men had been in a position to see the signal lights and all were supposed to be watching for them.

As for the crew of Via Rail No. 4, its members had also failed to brake, even though the approaching freight train was clearly visible before it reached the single track. They did not survive to answer why.

Investigators finally ascribed the disaster to human

error. Hudson and Edwards at the freight train's head end had failed to heed the signals, possibly because they were sleeping. Hudson, for example, had worked 26 of the previous 30 days and, along with Edwards, had already worked a graveyard shift before manning the ill-fated freight.

Conductor Smith may also have been fatigued. He'd taken the shift call on short notice only four hours after booking off his last shift. He later testified that the radios may have malfunctioned, even though he was able to use one immediately after the accident. Moreover, at least one was proven operable before the accident.

Smith also testified that, in his opinion, the speed of the freight train was appropriate, indicating no cause for alarm. He offered no explanation for failing to see the "prepare to stop" signal, but the Inquiry Board speculated that, at the time of the crash, he was not in the caboose's high cupola, where he should have been. Rather, it was put forward that he was at his more comfortable desk from which any signals would not be visible.

In this case, technology had done its job, but it could not make up for human error.

The Toronto Subway Wreck

On August 11, 1995, the evening rush hour in Toronto was nearly over. Traffic on the streets was returning to normal. Beneath the streets, rush hour was definitely petering out. Most subway passengers could now find seats. Lemmel

Layda was one of them, happy to sit as he headed home after his day's work as a waiter.

During peak periods, Toronto's 40-year-old subway system carried tens of thousands of people to work and home. One subway train could transport up to 2000 people at 80 kilometres per hour — 400-ton bullets.

That evening on the Spadina subway line, a southbound train carried a relatively small load, about 700 passengers. The train ran two red stop signals as it sped toward the Dupont station. On the track was an automatic mechanical brake, a backup for just this kind of situation. When the motorman failed to respond to the stop signals, the backup should have been triggered. It, too, failed — a result of poor maintenance.

Ahead was a second train, the reason for the red signals. It was fully stopped, waiting to be taken out of service for the night. Just 30 metres away, the southbound train raced through the darkness toward it. Layda had settled into his seat in the front car and was dozing.

With a grinding scream of crashing metal, the southbound train ploughed nearly six metres into the obstruction, heaving its rear end so high that it was jammed tightly against the tunnel ceiling. Pieces of wreckage blocked the tunnel from floor to ceiling and from side to side. Dust clouds belched into the closest stations and erupted up into the street through the ventilation shafts. Immediately, to prevent fire, officials in the subway control centre cut power to the tunnel. Now, except for a few dim emergency lights, ghostly darkness enveloped the scene.

The loud crash was followed by momentary ominous silence. Then, the moans and screams of injured and trapped passengers echoed up and down the tunnel. Layda later recounted those first moments from his hospital bed, severely injured. "The car I was in was crushed like a tin can. I tried to help a woman but all I could see were her legs." Unable to help her, Layda stumbled clear, where he was found by a rescuer and shepherded to the surface on a stretcher.

Rescuers quickly descended, following the cries of passengers through the dust-clogged dimness. They began guiding passengers to the escape tunnels. Others provided medical aid to the injured passengers. Then more rescuers arrived, wielding pry bars and cutting torches to free those trapped in the tangle of steel. With the ventilation system shut down, rescuers were forced to work in stifling 40-degree-Celsius temperatures throughout the night.

A veteran firefighter, Captain Paul Fitzgerald, led the second rescue team to arrive on the scene. He commended the dedication, energy, and professionalism of his team, whose rescue efforts continued without respite until midnight. Of his team and himself he said, "If they stopped working, they'd start thinking. I have enough nightmares already."

The motorman, although seriously injured, survived, never to drive a subway train again. Three passengers were not so fortunate. Two were pronounced dead at the scene and another died shortly after being admitted to hospital. Her story is particularly devastating. Severely injured and trapped in the wreckage for hours with her life in the balance, she was finally freed only after surgeons were forced to amputate her legs.

Before official inquiries and coroners' inquests were completed, the Toronto Transit Commission had already implemented 40 changes that were later recommended by the inquiries. All of these related to years of neglected maintenance and lack of training, both considered direct causes of the disaster. In the ensuing years, many of the additional 60 recommendations were also implemented. Sadly, the lives of three passengers, and the injuries of dozens of other people, were the impetus needed for change.

Chapter 5
The High Price of Coal

Coal fuelled the home furnaces and engines of industry in the 19th and early 20th centuries just as oil and natural gas do today. Canada was forged in the heat of a coal fire, with coal coming from British Columbia, Alberta, Saskatchewan, and Nova Scotia. Yet successfully tearing the soft black rock from below the earth's surface has come at a high price — a price paid in lives.

Coal mines have always been hazardous places, and coal mining is considered one of the most dangerous occupations in the world. The mines are infamous for their deadly methane and carbon monoxide gases. Both gases are odourless, and methane is extremely volatile. A spark can set it off. Add, then, accumulations of explosive, powdery coal dust in the air and along mine shafts, and the mine becomes a virtual powder keg.

The mines themselves are usually honeycombs of hollows beneath thousands of tons of rock. Every metre of tunnel increases the pressure from the rock above. The rock shifts, seeking its own level. Miners call these shifts "bumps." Sometimes bumps are welcome. They loosen coal, making it easier to mine.

Other times, however, bumps cause mine ceilings and walls to collapse or floors to heave up. Bumps can also release centuries-old pockets of methane or fill shafts with clouds of coal dust. In the worst cases, bumps tear up track and air pressure lines, smash steel coal cars and heavy equipment, and tear out live electrical wire. The sparks that sometimes result can send an explosive fireball throughout the mine's entire workings, sucking up oxygen and leaving behind carbon monoxide — "afterdamp," as the miners call it.

The Pictou County Coal Field

Ten thousand years before European settlers arrived in the Maritimes, Native peoples called Pictou County and the region around it *agg piktuk*, which, roughly translated, means "the explosive place." Likely, none of the miners working the Drummond Coal Mine in Pictou County knew this. If they did, they probably didn't care. Whatever its hazards, coal mining was their livelihood.

The Drummond Coal Mine was considered to be one

of the finest in Nova Scotia. The mine manager, James Dunn, personally carried out gas checks daily and was thought to be one of the best in the business. Coal mining ran in his family.

On May 13, 1873, his two sons were working a shift in the mine. That day, near the end of a shaft deep in the mine, a small fire started when Robert McLeod, the worker in charge of setting explosives, set off a charge to loosen coal. Such small fires were not uncommon, but this one soon got out of control.

Explosions ripped through the mine. The second of these blew flames, rock, timbers, and men out of every opening. Witnesses estimated flaming debris flew 200 metres into the air. So severe was the blast that an adjacent worked-out mine, which had been sealed, also blew wide open. The explosions and fires scoured every underground hollow space. After the first explosion, Dunn rushed into the mine. The next explosion killed him instantly. His sons also died.

Shattered beyond recovery, the Drummond Coal Mine was sealed, a mass grave for 60 men and boys.

The miners in the Drummond Mine were not the first to die in the Pictou County coal field, nor were they the last. By the end of 1952, the county's mines had claimed 244 lives in explosions. Many other fatalities also occurred due to sudden rock falls, asphyxiation, floods, inadequate equipment, and a myriad of other reasons. By the 1990s, however, the price of coal was high enough that investors were again eyeing the untapped lode in Pictou.

Against the advice of many experts, the federal and

provincial governments issued operating permits, purchase orders, and subsidies to Curragh Resources to mine coal from the Pictou fields, despite the fact that Curragh had no one in its management with coal mining experience. Their mine was called Westray, and it would work the Foord Seam — the scene of eight explosions since 1838, including one in 1918 that killed 88 miners.

At first, it was planned that the latest in technology would be employed in the new mine. However, to keep costs down and production high, it wasn't. Plans to implement the latest in safety measures also fell through. Indeed, many basic safety measures, known for decades to be essential, were either ignored or fell short of standards — this, in perhaps Canada's most dangerous coal field.

On Saturday, May 9, 1992, at 5:18 a.m., an explosion caused by excessive accumulations of methane gas and coal dust ripped through the Westray workings, killing 26 miners.

As can often happen when the ambitious — and perhaps ill-conceived — plans of corporate and government interests go awry, the efforts of survivors and victims' families to obtain redress faced a long uphill battle. To date, aspects of the Westray disaster are still periodically before the courts.

Springhill's Mines
Throughout the latter half of the 1950s, the people of Springhill, Nova Scotia, came to know firsthand the omni-

present peril of coal mines. It began in 1956, when runaway coal carts snapped a live power cable, setting off a coal dust explosion. Gas generated by the explosion seeped throughout the mine, slowing rescue attempts.

Springhill's local physician, Arnold Burden, faced the horror head-on. Although he'd never been down in the mines, he bravely descended into the gas-filled mine to provide assistance underground. The first three fatalities he saw were former schoolmates.

Far below Burden, at the 1800-metre level, the air contained enough gas that it could have killed the handful of survivors trapped there. Fortunately, they'd managed to punch holes in a compressed air hose and breathe through that while awaiting rescue.

Burden knew the men were still alive, but he also knew that the gas was causing sporadic fires, any one of which could erupt through the workings. Inching his way along, he struck a pocket of gas and passed out.

Draegermen, miners trained in underground rescues, revived Burden, whose first thoughts, recorded later in his journal, were, "My God, I'm down here and if I don't make it back up I've got a wife and children who will have nothing ... I'm not even being paid!" Putting those thoughts aside, Burden resumed the search.

Several hours later, the courageous doctor and the draegermen finally reached the trapped miners. Burden was among the last handful of men who emerged from the mine, which was then sealed to starve the fires of oxygen. In total, 88 miners were rescued, but 39 died. Despite the tragedy, coal mining in Springhill continued.

Springhill's Cumberland No. 2 coal mine was the deepest in North America — a straight drop of 1450 metres, with nearly 6.5 kilometres of tunnels that branched from the core, following coal veins in all directions. The mine had opened in 1873, the same year the Drummond mine closed.

On October 23, 1958, 174 workers were in No. 2's depths. Around 8 p.m., well into the afternoon shift, the mine was shaken by a bump so severe it registered on seismographs in Ottawa 1100 kilometres away. The upheaval pushed tunnel floors into ceilings in an instant. It was cataclysmic for the men underground. While there was no fire or explosion, the deadly methane was so thick in the air that it extinguished rescuers' lamps. In some sections of the mine, breathing apparatuses were all that kept rescuers alive.

Once again, Burden made his way to the scene with the draegermen. Forty-five hundred metres into No. 2, draegermen found men still alive. One, Leon Melanson, was buried under a coal fall with only part of his shoulders and face exposed. As rescuers chipped at the coal to free him, they discovered he was also trapped by a leg across his chest. They asked Burden to amputate the leg — assuming it belonged to a dead miner — in order to free Melanson. But Burden pleaded for patience, correctly suspecting that the leg was Melanson's own, despite its impossible angle. The rescuers resumed their work, uncovering the man coal by coal. Later at the hospital, the doctor attempted to save the leg, but was unsuccessful.

Tunnels had collapsed, compressing fallen rock, shoring, and equipment into some passages. Other tunnels were completely blocked. Nevertheless, rescuers brought 81 miners out of the darkness in the first two days of searching. But, on October 25, mine management announced that it feared there were no more survivors.

The draegermen persisted, if only to account for all the men in the mine. On October 29, six days after the bump, draegermen who were clearing wreckage heard a voice. It was faint and fragmented. Behind the wreckage, deeper in the shaft, trapped men had heard a shovel scrape against a pipe. One of them, Gorley Kempt, shouted down the pipe, "We're alive in here. There are 12 of us!" Rescuers began frantically digging through 28 metres of coal and rubble to reach them, finally breaking through the next day.

A second miracle occurred on the ninth day, when another miner was discovered alive, followed shortly by six more. The seven men came to be known as Springhill's Group of Seven. They had spent nine days trapped 4300 metres below the surface. Originally, there'd been eight, but Percy Rector had died from his injuries. The seven who remained were Frank Hunter, Doug Jewkes, Garnett Clarke, Currie Smith, Herb Pepperdine, Barney Martin, and Maurice Ruddick — the last man to leave alive.

John Calder was one of the rescuers. His conversation with Ruddick is recorded in the CBC archives as follows:

"Ruddick? You in there, Maurice?" Calder called.

"I'm here," he heard back.

"Man, the workmen's compensation board sent me specifically down here to get you out."

"Why is that?" Ruddick asked.

"Why," said Calder, "they said they'd have to pay so much to your wife and 12 children, if we don't find you, there won't be enough left over for the others."

While humour, even if cynical or macabre, could sometimes buffer miners from their dangerous reality, in the town of Springhill that day there was little joy. Families were left to mourn 75 miners.

Today, thousands of tons of coal lie beneath Springhill. The town's last mine, No. 2, was officially closed in 1959, putting 1000 miners out of work. In less than a century, Springhill's coal had cost 239 lives. The price in pain, sorrow, and danger was finally deemed too high.

Yet, Springhill and the other coal mines of the eastern Maritimes were not the most dangerous. Mining experts gave that distinction to the coal mines of British Columbia and Alberta, and not without justification. Between 1892 and 1901, in the western mines, there were 6.6 fatalities for every million tons of coal. In Great Britain the comparable rate was .614 and in the Pennsylvania coal fields, the rate was .415.

Tragedy in the Crowsnest Pass

As the transcontinental railway was being built through the Crowsnest Pass, a remote, rugged region that straddles the southern British Columbia/Alberta border, vast quantities of coal were discovered. By the turn of the 20th century, coal mines dotted the area.

Bellevue was a small but prosperous mine on the Alberta side of the pass — that is, until December 9, 1910. That was the day a sudden explosion trapped 47 men. Fellow miners attempted rescue, despite the fact that the mine had no rescue equipment. Members of one rescue team were overcome by gas and had to be rescued themselves. One rescuer, Fred Alderson, gave his own air tank and helmet to another who needed them. On his way back to the surface, Alderson succumbed to carbon monoxide.

The most significant aspect of this disaster was the fate of 21 men brought out alive but unconscious from carbon monoxide poisoning. None recovered, partly, as a *Calgary Herald* editorial suggested, because the necessary emergency medical equipment had not been available at the scene.

The Bellevue disaster positively changed the safety conditions of coal mining in the Crowsnest. This was clearly demonstrated on June 19, 1914, at the Hillcrest Mine, also on the Alberta side of the pass.

The Hillcrest mine was one of the best producers in the Crowsnest. It was also one of the safest. Methane levels were tested several times a day, at least once every shift. At

7 a.m. on June 19, tests showed the gas level to be well below five percent (the level at which it can poison men and/or explode). Two and a half hours later, the mine blew apart with such force that two men working outside were killed instantly. Fuelled by the gas and then the coal dust, explosion after explosion wracked the mine.

Rescue operations began immediately. Veteran miners knew that any workers not killed by the explosions could be killed by the afterdamp. In the first few minutes after the mine quieted, 19 men managed to escape. Rescuers quickly found 3 more. They were working against the clock — the afterdamp was filling every shaft.

Hillcrest had rescue and resuscitation equipment on-site. By 10 a.m., more had arrived from nearby communities. Supervised by Dr. William Dodd, the resuscitation equipment was set up in a makeshift tent near the mine head.

Before noon, rescuers had managed to penetrate through debris to reach almost every part of the mine. In one section, they found several men who had soaked their shirts in water to filter their air. They were unconscious. Joe Atkinson was among them. He required three hours of resuscitation before he finally came to. The next day, he was back in the mine searching fruitlessly for his comrades. Late that morning, the last seven survivors were brought out of the mine. It was a month before the second last body was brought out. The body of one miner was never found.

The stories of many of the victims were, not surprisingly,

tragic. Rod Wallis and William Neath had been wrapping up their last shift before returning to Nova Scotia to take up farming. They didn't make it. In another case, two of three brothers working the morning shift died. Most tragic, perhaps, was the courageous attempt by David Murray to rescue his three sons. Having barely survived himself, he pushed past security guards and re-entered the mine to try to find his sons. He soon became a victim of the afterdamp. His sons, by then, were already dead.

Some men scheduled to work that fateful shift were lucky. Two were sent home because the timekeeper smelled liquor on their breath. Steve Belopotsky had switched from the morning shift to help out a friend. Another miner had called in sick simply because he didn't feel like working on a Friday. He'd already had two days off and wanted to enjoy an uninterrupted holiday until Monday.

The Hillcrest disaster is still relatively unknown. Steven Hanon, who recently created a documentary on the subject, *The Devil's Breath,* expressed frustration at the reticence of people in the area. "I think there was a genuine reluctance by family members and friends in the Crowsnest Pass to talk about this," he said. "It reminded miners of their own vulnerability. It was too painful for the survivors. It just became a buried part of our history."

In terms of loss of life — 189 men in all — however, Hillcrest is the worst mining disaster in Canadian history. One hundred and thirty of the miners left widows to raise

400 children. Julia Elliah was one of the widows. A decade before, a few kilometres away at Frank, Alberta, her husband, Bill, had barely survived another historic catastrophe when he was trapped in a mine beneath Turtle Mountain as a result of the 1903 Frank Slide.

According to early Native peoples in the area, Turtle Mountain was the "mountain that walks." To them, the mountain suggested danger, and it was avoided. This danger, however, was of no interest to businessman H.L. Frank, and in 1901 he opened a coal mine between the base of the mountain and the Old Man River. To house his workers, he built a small town across the river beside the Canadian Pacific Railway tracks. He named his town Frank.

For two years, miners dug into Turtle Mountain. Because the seam was wide, they used the "pillar and stall" method to create a drift mine. This type of mining involved digging huge rooms (stalls) and leaving natural rock pillars to support the ceiling. The mine extended 700 metres into the mountain.

While it didn't exactly walk, Turtle Mountain periodically shook itself awake. Frequent vibrations loosened coal in the stalls, and mining became little more than shovelling the ore that had fallen from ceilings into carts. However, at 4:10 a.m. on April 29, 1903, Turtle Mountain finally walked.

With a crash that was heard 160 kilometres away, 100 million tons of Turtle Mountain's eastern slope broke away and plunged into the valley below. The compressed air, which the mountain of rock pushed ahead of it, flattened houses, tents, and mine buildings. The slide that followed then buried them. The Old Man River did not slow the onslaught, nor did the CPR mainline that ran on the far side of town. The slide ran over both. Within 90 seconds, the rock slide, 2.5 kilometres wide, had swept almost 5 kilometres across the valley and up the other side.

Inside the mine, miners were still alive. They had already ascertained the impossibility of digging through to the mine's entrance, 100 metres of tunnel packed solid with rubble. Instead, they retreated deeper and began digging a vertical tunnel. The problem was lack of oxygen. The slide had destroyed the ventilation system and sealed the miners from outside air. They were, they realized, living on borrowed time.

Finally, 13 hours after the slide, the men emerged. They were stunned by the devastation. Their own ordeal forgotten, they almost immediately pitched in to look for survivors.

Fortunately, most of the town was outside the slide's path, although just barely. A few houses and an itinerant miners' camp along the edge of the slide were not so lucky. They were both crushed.

The Leitch family home was among those destroyed. The father, the mother, and four of the family's seven children died. At first, the youngest Leitch daughter, infant Marion, could not be found. The next day, she was located some distance from her demolished house, nestled unscathed in a hay bale that could only have blown from the livery stable, half a kilometre away.

In the end, 26 people were known to be dead, although only 12 bodies were ever recovered. It's thought that the death toll may have been higher. Some have guessed that 50 or more men may have been camped in the valley where the slide occurred, which would have brought the toll to 70 or more, but this has never been confirmed.

H.L. Frank was in Paris at the time. Only a few days before the slide, he had finalized the sale of the mine to a French consortium.

Chapter 6
Fire!

any disasters are limited in their immediate impact in the sense that they suddenly and directly affect a determinable number of people in a limited geographic area. Other disasters, however, are much more geographically widespread, impacting cities, towns, and even the country — to the point that a core collective strength is required to enable recovery. Many of these powerful, devastating disasters have involved fire.

The Great Fire of 1916
By the early 1900s, rail lines had been carved deep into northern Ontario. Homesteaders had pushed north to clear forests edging the tracks, and lumberjacks had followed, pushing even deeper into the wilderness. As the rock was uncovered,

new wealth was discovered — gold, silver, and nickel. The rail lines were clogged with freight trains hauling timber and minerals south, and prospectors north.

Small ramshackle towns sprang up along the Temiskaming and Northern Ontario Railway. They had names like Porcupine, Timmins, Cobalt, Cochrane, Haileybury, Pottsville, Englehardt, New Liskeard, and Matheson. Some, like New Liskeard, served farmers, while others served the miners and lumberjacks. So many little towns dotted the landscape that the area soon resembled the Cariboo and Klondike during the gold rush days.

To the weathered sourdoughs who had come from those distant gold fields, northern Ontario had some similarities they'd have preferred to avoid. Winter cold could be as deadly as it was in Dawson. During the summer, as the old stories go, men in the bush would slather themselves with bear grease to ward off black flies and mosquitoes, then sizzle in relentless heat waves like bacon on a griddle.

Summer also brought the threat of forest fires, fuelled by tinder dry vegetation, stiff steady winds, wooden and canvas buildings, and trains with red-hot fireboxes. Fire prevention was no more than a well and a pail on a rope. The people of Cochrane, Ontario, boasted a fire apparatus with a pressurized hose. Along the rail lines, one firefighter was hired to patrol every 40 kilometres of track. He was given a handcar, a shovel, and an axe to extinguish brush fires caused by sparks from passing trains.

Fire!

The gold town of Porcupine was two years old in 1911 when a forest fire levelled it, along with 260,000 hectares of brush and forest. Three thousand people, many of them miners, were left homeless. The wealth of the region was too rich a lure to be abandoned, however, and the people rebuilt. Despite the danger, fire was still used to clear brush for construction and farming, much as it is used today in South American rain forests. Railroad section hands routinely set fires to clear encroaching brush from track beds. All the while, train engines continued to billow hot embers as they passed the moisture-starved forests of jackpine and spruce.

July of 1916 was a scorcher in northern Ontario, the air so thick with heat that just breathing was hard work. On July 29, the wind picked up, adding dust to the heat haze. Before breakfast dishes were cleared, the wind was gusting across the Matheson area, carrying the faint odour of burning wood, presumably, as local people thought, from controlled slash fire — homesteaders clearing land or rail section crews cutting back brush so dense and prolific it could overgrow the track.

But this smoke did not come from a controlled fire. It began beside a rail line in moisture-starved thickets of juniper and jack pine seedlings, the result of a migrant spark from the funnel of a passing freight train. The gusting wind was all that it needed to fan into an inferno.

By noon, the sky over Matheson had darkened across the horizon, an advancing wall of deep grey that forced fierce winds ahead of it. Rain would have been welcome, except these were not rain clouds. The wind did the rest, consolidating the fires from tree crowns to roots, becoming an inferno, building its own winds, feeding on oxygen, heat, and flame like a tidal wave too fast to outrun, too powerful to resist.

Sparks blown on the wind set the town on fire before the main blaze even reached it. The flames sped on without pause, catching a freight train that had slowed to pick up people fleeing the fire. To escape, the train had to break through the flames. But before it could, the superheated fire exploded two freight cars. Desperate homesteaders leaped from the burning cars, uncoupled them, then ran back through the flames to clamber aboard the train.

The fire grew as the afternoon wore on. Matheson was incinerated, followed by Cochrane, Iroquois Falls, Timmins, and a score of small enclaves in between. Cochrane became a funeral pyre. Water in the town's new fire hose turned to steam just before the hose ignited.

Unable to outrun the fire, people sought refuge. At one whistle stop along the rail line, Reverend Wilfrid Gagne tried to shelter 35 parishioners in a clay hut. The heat, as the fire burned through the community, was too much and almost everyone suffocated.

Just outside Matheson, Frank Monahan quickly managed to fashion some scaffolding in his well. Three families huddled inside as the fire passed over. By repeatedly pouring water over them with his hat, Monahan saved everyone but a small child.

That night, with little left to burn, the fire began to peter out. In Matheson, only three houses were left standing. On a rail siding, two steel cars loaded with coal were burnt out, and yet, hooked up between them, two wooden cars loaded with combustible goods were unscathed — not even scorched. The town's wood flagpole still stood tall, although a rope had burned right through, dropping the flag to half-mast.

During the next day, torrential rains turned the ash into 200,000 hectares of pasty, foul-smelling soot. The sifting for bodies had already begun. Smoke inhalation and suffocation had killed many. Root cellars had become sealed ovens, sucked dry of oxygen. Some wells had become cauldrons. Groups of people had died while trying to find shelter in clearings. Officially, 223 people had succumbed, but the number of people cremated in a fire so hot it left no trace could not be counted.

Graves were dug in cemeteries thickly coated in ash. Survivors worked robotically, deeply shocked. For days afterward, they spoke sparingly to one another, their voices hoarse and raspy — too much stinging smoke and searing heat had assaulted their throats and lungs.

These were tough people, though. Eventually the shock wore off. Shanty and tent towns grew up again along the rail lines. The mines reopened. Before winter, gold and silver bumped southward on the long freights, and prospectors crammed the otherwise empty cars returning north for more. In 1916, northern Ontario was still a frontier. Hardship —

even disaster — was to be expected in the rough-and-tumble life in which extremes were the norm.

The land, too, proved hardy. Before the first snow, vegetation had sprouted throughout the region. The next year, homesteaders reported bumper crops in the New Liskeard area.

Canadian Identity Ablaze

About 660 kilometres to the southeast of Matheson lay Ottawa, the nation's capital. Here, Canada's monuments to its civility, democracy, and strength — the symbols of a great nation and the seat of its national government — were established. The Gothic majesty of the Parliament Buildings, perched high on the hills overlooking the Ottawa River, attested to all that was fine about the nation. Unfortunately, fire shows as little respect for the works of great architects as it does for the rundown buildings of a shantytown.

On the cold winter night of February 3, 1916, fire made its immutable point. The Centre Block of the Parliament Buildings was a soaring stone edifice crowned by the Victoria Clock Tower. From this building, the parliamentarians of the House of Commons legislated Canada's future. That night, the House was in session, debating fish marketing. But the fish were quickly forgotten when, just before 9 p.m., Frank Glass, a member of parliament, dashed into the Commons Chamber to report that the building was on fire. The deputy speaker quickly rose and left the room.

By then, corridors were filling with smoke. The members

wasted no time evacuating. Prime Minister Robert Borden was whisked to safety via a back stairway. Once outside, he had to borrow a coat and hat. A brisk north wind swirling over Parliament Hill had plunged the temperature to well below zero.

The quick arrival of firefighters couldn't save the House of Commons. Its roof caved in within half an hour of the blaze's discovery. The Senate chamber was next. In the meantime, two MPs had been forced to climb down from a washroom window on a rope hastily tied together using towels.

Other people were not so fortunate. Two guests of the house speaker died in a corridor when they returned to the building to retrieve their coats. The member of parliament for Yarmouth, the Honourable B.B. Law, was found dead near the Reading Room, where Glass had discovered the fire. Weakened by fire and the weight of the collapsed roof, a wall crashed down upon three other men, one of whom was a police officer. A seventh victim was found in the ruins two days later. This man, frightened of heights, had hoped his friend would send rescuers to his second floor window because he'd feared to jump. Unfortunately, his friend had knocked himself unconscious when he'd leapt to safety and had not recovered in time to tell rescuers of the man's predicament.

National Library employees sealed their building in an effort to save its irreplaceable contents. With the help of firefighters, who saturated the exterior with water, their efforts succeeded. In the Centre Block, former prime minister Wilfrid Laurier's office was gutted. Lost within it were all his historic personal records.

Eventually the wind shifted the fire away from the library, allowing its insatiable fury, instead, to attack the Victoria Clock Tower atop the Centre Block. The tower began to burn at 11 p.m. At midnight, the clock failed to strike and, at 1:20 a.m., the tower collapsed.

After the first hour, the greatest danger was not inside the buildings. Outside, the thousands of gallons of water that had been poured onto the buildings froze to every surface — firefighters, police officers, and soldiers included. The men were caught between fire and ice. Many required treatment for frostbite, while others broke limbs after slipping on ice. Exploding glass sprayed like shrapnel. Despite these hazards, the fire was arrested by 3 a.m.

In the light of dawn on a cold, clear morning, with wind still whipping across Parliament Hill, the extent of the damage emerged. The Centre Block stood like a maimed, silent spectre. Most of its exterior walls had held, although they were so weakened they later had to be demolished. The skeleton was coated in a shroud of ice, except for the deep-set arched windows. These gaped, filled only by the wind that howled through gutted corridors and chambers.

Sir Robert Borden, it turned out, could return the borrowed coat and hat. His own had escaped harm, still hanging on the coat stand in his office. His desk and the papers upon it were also untouched. The rest of his office, however, was destroyed.

That Canada's Parliament Buildings, monuments to nationhood and durability, could be transformed to ruin in a few hours was a shock to the country. The fire had occurred at the height of the Great War, and passions ran high. Sabotage was suspected, but officials moved quickly to quell the rumour.

An immediate investigation suggested that Canada's Parliament Buildings were victims of their own grandeur. No expense had been spared installing dry pine woodwork, nor covering the panels and doors with coat after coat of flammable varnish. Throughout the buildings, the shellacked wooden floors gleamed with multiple coats of oil or paste wax. Only the National Library had steel doors. At the time, while warehouses and office buildings had sprinkler systems and many of the country's slum tenements had fire escapes, Canada's seat of power had neither.

When it was ruled that the fire was accidental, the desire to rebuild — stronger and more magnificently — took hold across the country. Today's Parliament buildings may appear much the same on the outside as the originals, but inside they are fitted with alarm and sprinkler systems, more fire exits, and far fewer combustible materials. Firewalls now protect offices and chambers, ensuring that any fire can be contained until extinguished.

Vancouver's Great Fire

Even entire Canadian cities have not been exempt from fire. In 1877, St. John, New Brunswick, vanished. In 1892, two-thirds of St. John's, Newfoundland, was gutted. In 1898, in New Westminster, British Columbia, only the city jail was saved — by its prisoners. In 1904, in Toronto, 98 downtown buildings were destroyed. And in 1907 and 1910, in Victoria, one fire destroyed more than 100 houses, and the second blazed through the city's retail core.

In 1886, it was Vancouver's turn. At the time, the city was still a motley collection of tents and rough-framed wooden shops. Although fortunes were being made from railway building and the lumber trade, they were being spent in Victoria and New Westminster. The workers lived in Vancouver, but the town had more ambitious aspirations, partly because it was a better commercial port than New Westminster and not isolated on an island like Victoria. Moreover, the railroad was being pushed from New Westminster, its initial terminus, to Burrard Inlet. That could only mean prosperity for Vancouver.

By early afternoon on Sunday, June 13, God-fearing folk had returned to their homes from church services. Hungover lumberjacks, stevedores, and fishermen were either recounting their fuzzy memories of the night before or imbibing more of the dog that bit them.

The populace of Vancouver was clustered on the south shore of Burrard Inlet, a probe of the Pacific Ocean that had created the city's harbour. Surrounding the inlet were low hills, once forested, but now shorn of trees, cut down to build the town's wharves and shanties. The brush, however, had continued to grow on these hills — dense, waist-high, and impenetrable. Added to that was dead brush, cleared and piled to facilitate easier access to trees with commercial value, and to clear a right of way for the much-anticipated rail line.

How the fire started, no one knows for sure. But everyone in town instantly knew it had started in that hillside brush. They knew, too, that it was massive, uncontrollable, and rushing down the hills toward them.

Warnings rang out — not to muster a defence, but to flee. Burrard Inlet filled with boats, rafts, and anything else that floated. To all these, people desperately clung. One unidentified man who saved himself by grabbing a plank and flutter-kicking his way offshore summed up the fire by saying, "The buildings simply melted before the fiery blast."

It was over in 2 hours; indeed, some eyewitnesses said, in 20 minutes. Vancouver was reduced to seven buildings and a smouldering shoreline. Nearly 1200 people were left homeless. Eight were confirmed dead, but the death toll was probably higher. Many people in Vancouver were transients with neither friends nor family to ask after them. As well, the intense heat of the fire was such that bodies would have been incinerated as if in a crematorium.

Before dusk that day, stunned survivors walked in the ruins, ash still smouldering, homes and possessions long gone. One woman had rescued her sewing machine and with that sewed together a modest livelihood in future days. In a photograph taken three days after the fire, the town councillors and the mayor are posing outside their temporary headquarters — a tent with a hand-painted wooden sign, slightly askew, that says, "City Hall." Their dignity leaves no doubt of the town's will to recover.

Within five years the railroad had arrived. Vancouver's population soared to 15,000. By then the ambitious resurrected city was planning a tramline, certainly a sign that the fire was put behind them.

Chapter 7
From Sea to Shore

or generations, Canadians have endured inclement, often extreme, weather on a regular basis. Generally, they take a hard-nosed frontier approach to it. "It comes with the territory," they say resignedly, then continue with their daily routines, confident that whatever the elements may throw their way, they will overcome it. Sometimes, however, this characteristic Canadian confidence can be severely tested — even shaken.

Ocean Tremors
In 1929, an event occurred along Newfoundland's Burin Peninsula that devastated most of the outports along its coast in less than a minute. At that time, the majority of

the outports along the southern peninsula were tiny fishing villages perched on rocky shores. Many had been there for almost as long as men had fished the Grand Banks. Inhabitants of these settlements were accustomed to perils at sea. Not for a minute, however, did they think that peril from the sea might reach out for them on dry land.

On November 18, 1929, at about 5 p.m., all this changed. A roar, similar to the sound of a massive explosion, thundered through the outports. The ground shook, shop goods tumbled from shelves, and cupboards in homes burst open, spilling dishes and supplies onto the floor. Whatever it was, it soon passed, and it wasn't long before the water in the bays was once again glassy calm.

St. Lawrence Harbour shopkeeper George Bartlett later recalled villagers gathering to speculate about the event, but they were baffled. "Eventually," he said, "they went home to tea." Bartlett and his assistants spent the next little while putting everything back together in his shop.

What they didn't realize was that nearly 250 kilometres to the south, the ocean floor had convulsed as a result of an earthquake measuring 7.2 on the Richter scale. The people of Burin Peninsula had no idea what was coming.

Before 5:30 p.m., a tsunami — the tidal wave resulting from the earthquake — was racing toward the peninsula and its unsuspecting inhabitants. Within two hours of the earthquake, some witnesses noticed the water level in the harbour suddenly drop. In St. Lawrence, the harbour, normally under 10 metres of water, was now exposed. Almost immediately, the tsunami struck. From the bare harbour, water rose to 30 metres. The first wave was followed by two more, as the same horror crashed upon outports for 110 kilometres along the peninsula.

Bartlett was visiting a steamer moored in St. Lawrence harbour. By the time he dashed out onto the deck, the ship had been carried over the wharf and was already surrounded by floating houses, shattered fish-drying racks, and other debris. He soon discovered that his shop, a substantial 10-metre-high building, was gone. Later, he found it inland, on a patch of meadow, his stock undisturbed. Such was the force of the great wave.

One man was drawn inland by the wave, then, buoyed by a chicken coop, was cast back into the harbour when it receded. He saw a floating house and swam to it for safety, realizing as he climbed through a window that it was his own.

On the second floor of another floating house, rescuers found a sleeping baby. On the main floor, they found the baby's mother and three other children, all drowned.

At Kelly's Cove, recalled Pearl Brushett, then five years old, the first wave drove the Brushett family home across the harbour to the far shore, while the second wave carried them back to the village side. Her mother managed to rescue all five children.

Marian Kelly, then just 11, rescued her younger brother

by leaping a fence to higher ground. Safe, she turned around and watched helplessly as her mother, her sister, and their house were swept away with the receding wave. Later, in shock, she could only say, "It took everything when it came."

Forty villages along the coast were ravaged. More than 500 buildings and 125 boats were destroyed. Amazingly, only 28 people lost their lives, although four years later, in 1933, the tsunami claimed a 29th life when a victim died of lingering complications from injuries.

Rescue and relief came slowly. The Burin Peninsula had no roads, nor, at the time, any way to communicate with the outside world. It took two long days to transmit a wireless message requesting assistance. During that time, fierce gales and near blizzard conditions pounded the ruins.

By the time relief began to arrive, the situation was desperate. Food supplies had been destroyed, medical supplies exhausted, and even blankets were scarce. At that time, the government had no formal role in disaster relief. Nor did it have anything remotely similar to the tightly meshed social safety net Canadians know today. Victims of disasters were dependent on the charity of their neighbours. Fortunately, the outpouring of public support, organized through hospitals, newspapers, steamship companies, and merchants, was fast and effective.

The next spring, fishermen on the peninsula still managed to muster their regular sealing fleet. However, the tsunami had disrupted the commercial fishery industry on the Grand Banks when its passage had scoured the seabed. Recovery took another two years, another hardship that the people of the Burin Peninsula outports managed to overcome.

An Unexpected Hurricane

It was October 15, 1954. For days, the Toronto area had been deluged with rain. Commuters cursed the inconvenience during rush hour traffic, but, they reasoned, rain was better than snow, and the snow would be coming soon enough. So, grumbling aside, they put up with it.

The previous day, Torontonians who owned televisions would have seen the report of a hurricane named Hazel that was sweeping up the east coast of the United States. Most would have guessed that a few remnants of the storm would hit the city, typically bringing some windiness for a day, plus more rain. These hurricanes normally blew themselves out against the Allegheny Mountains in upstate New York, if not sooner.

Hurricane Hazel, however, changed direction slightly, sidestepped the Alleghenies, and charged across Lake Ontario, picking up more moisture as she went. Hazel was the first Category 4 hurricane (on a scale of 1 to 5) to strike Canada and, to date, the only one.

By this time, Toronto had already spread out across whatever land it could develop for industry and housing. To the west, Toronto's suburbs sprawled beyond the Humber River. Snuggled scenically along the Humber's shores — on its flood plain, in fact — was Raymore Drive, an enclave of comfortable single-family houses. The scenic, serene Humber had great appeal to home buyers. Even though the river occasionally ran high and fast during spring runoff, it had never been a problem.

On the night of October 15, that all changed as Hurricane Hazel reached Canada. In less than 24 hours, she dumped 300 million tons of water on the Toronto area. Every river, creek, and meandering brook within 60 kilometres of the city ran rampant. The normally docile Humber River ran amok, tearing out bridges and washing out roads all along its course. A swing bridge just upriver from Raymore Drive was ripped from its abutments. Fatefully, its debris altered the course of the Humber ever so slightly, enough for the river to pour its waters straight across the Raymore Drive section of the flood plain.

In less than an hour of being merely windswept and rain soaked, Raymore Drive was overwhelmed by a 20-foot-high current of raging water, "thundering like a freight train" as it tore the cozy homes from their foundations in the cold, black dead of night. Sixteen houses, two of them duplexes, were swept away in the malevolent waters. Thirty-six residents of Raymore Drive died.

Across the region that night, firefighters saved dozens of lives. Alex Nicholson was one of the lucky ones. He had been driving through the storm when his car swirled off a road and into the Don River. After five and a half hours gripping a tree, he was finally rescued by firefighters. Unable to get a line to him through the gusting wind, they had formed a human chain to draw him to safety.

Firefighters — unfamiliar with the ferocity of a storm like Hazel — were also caught themselves. The men of the Kingsway-Lambton Volunteer Fire Department were among them. That night, an eight-man crew headed along a road paralleling the Humber River in response to a call about people trapped on the roof of a car. The road ran in the bottom of a cut between a high, steep embankment and the river, which by this time was moving fast and rising quickly.

It wasn't long before the firetruck stalled as water rose above its wheel wells. As the force of the current picked up the heavy truck, the frightened firefighters, who had already climbed onto the roof of the cab, were forced to abandon the vehicle. Only two could swim. These two and another firefighter survived by grabbing tree branches and holding on until lines were cast to them and they were pulled to shore. Their five comrades were swept to their death.

Another drama that played out that night made the front page of the *Toronto Daily Star* the next day. The story was about a baby, four-month-old Nancy Thorpe, who was passed off to local firefighter Chief Albert Houston by her frantic mother. Before Houston was able to get back to the house to rescue Nancy's mother and the other occupants, the house was swept away by the fast-moving Etobicoke Creek.

Little Nancy was then passed from person to person

before she finally arrived in the arms of 16-year-old Sylvia Jones, secure on the roof of her father's house. For nearly six hours, Sylvia clutched the child, giving her up at dawn when rescuers finally came for her and 31 others.

Several days passed before Nancy was identified by relatives. It was then discovered that her parents, grandparents, and brother had all been lost in the storm. The only thing that remained of their house was the front steps.

The Thorpe family home wasn't the only one that floated off its foundations during that terrible night. The de Peuter family lived north of Toronto in a long, narrow valley known as the Holland Marsh. They were an immigrant family of 14 who had left Holland, ironically, because of the devastating floods in their own homeland. Living so far inland, they thought that another flood in their lives was inconceivable — but this was Holland Marsh. Although it had been drained for farming many years earlier, Hurricane Hazel brought back the marsh's water with a vengeance.

Over several hours, the de Peuters stayed in their new house as the water rose around them. Then, quite suddenly, around 2 a.m., the house drifted from its foundation. It floated through the marsh until 6:30 in the morning, when it ran aground in a carrot field. By this time, it had travelled four kilometres from its foundation and 75 metres from the nearest shore. Fortunately, the family escaped unharmed and the house remained remarkably intact.

It wasn't long before the provincial government and

Ontario Hydro stepped in to help Holland Marsh families such as the de Peuters. Within 29 days, enough equipment had been mobilized to pump the marsh dry again. The de Peuter family and many others were moved back to their land.

Disasters that have widespread, often tragic, impact on many people often have quirky asides that can soften the anguish of the moment. Betty Kennedy reported one such: an 82-year-old bedridden grandmother and her son rescued 27 cats and 14 dogs before they in turn were rescued by sea cadets. Lieutenant John Connor of the Royal Canadian Sea Cadet Corps *Ark Royal* reported that "not so much as a hiss, scratch, growl or bark occurred during the rescue. When we reached high ground near the Woodbridge fire hall, our cargo of cats and dogs were last seen heading for still higher ground, but still together." The grandmother was taken from her house bundled in quilts on her mattress.

Hurricane Hazel taught the people of southern Ontario many tough lessons. After the storm, flood plains were no longer used for housing development. Instead, they were turned into parks. Emergency response systems and early warning communication systems and regulations were both upgraded. Officials had learned the hard way that an early decision not to warn first responders and the general public of Hazel's potential had been a deadly one. Mistakes like that would not be made again.

Overall, 81 lives were lost across the region, and the

homeless numbered in the thousands. The potential for the Humber River to wreak similar damage in the future has been eliminated, and Holland Marsh will never again rise up to devastate its residents. Much of the Humber's flood plain is now a tourist attraction, and the waterways around the marsh are cloistered in flood-control dikes and levees.

A few years after Hurricane Hazel, the aftermath of Hurricane Diane tried its luck on Toronto. It made for a wet, windy day, but Torontonians endured — comfortably.

The Storm of '98

The winter of 1997–1998 brought a different type of weather disaster to Canadians from central Ontario all the way to Nova Scotia. The season started with rare mild temperatures. There was snow in December, but only enough to provide a traditional white Christmas. Then, on January 5, the rain began.

Meteorologists had multiple explanations for what occurred during the next five days. They claimed it had to do with low pressures over Texas, warm wet air from the Gulf of Mexico, high-pressure Arctic air over Hudson's Bay, and even El Niño causing a jetstream of sub-tropical air across the Gulf Coast of the U.S. By the evening rush hour in Canada's eastern cities, the people weren't much interested in *what* was causing the rain; they just wanted it to end.

They would have to wait a while.

Between January 5 and 10, rain fell for 80 hours, nearly

twice the annual accumulated total hours. As it fell, it froze. The area was steadily coated with an ever-thickening layer of ice. To walk from doorstep to street was to risk a broken leg or arm. Worse, the weight of the ice was snapping off tree branches without warning. The outdoors moaned a treacherous dirge of cracking flora.

By the second day of the storm, the weight of the ice began to bring down power and telephone lines, then the poles and transmission pylons. Hardware stores did a landslide business selling portable generators, to the point that convoys of semi-trailers were bringing them in from distant provinces and states. Flashlights and batteries were also stripped from store shelves, and barbecuing in the rain became trendy.

At its height, the Ice Storm of '98 left 4 million people without power, communication, or heat. Two weeks after the storm, 700,000 people were still without power, and another 100,000 were still living in shelters, unable to return to their homes. Miraculously, only 25 people died as a direct result of the storm, some from carbon monoxide poisoning when they tried heating with faulty fireplaces or gas-powered space heaters.

Sixteen thousand troops were rushed into the region to clear fallen trees and patrol rural areas that had been temporarily abandoned by residents. The families were forced into community centres converted into hostels, or into the homes of relatives and friends who were often in as dire straits. The dairy farms of western Quebec and eastern Ontario, principal suppliers to Canada's most populous area, were crippled. Desperate livestock farmers shared generators, trucking them from farm to farm over slick backroads. Armed forces and hydro personnel found elderly couples huddled in their remote houses, many faring remarkably well (by pioneer standards) and refusing to leave. Indeed, some were pleased to demonstrate survival skills learned in childhood — before central heat, refrigeration, running water, and electricity. Nevertheless, food rotted in refrigerators and freezers, and grocery stores were closed — not that it mattered, because so were the banks. Only a few main roads were passable, and their use was restricted to emergency personnel and supply convoys.

The Montreal area was particularly hard hit. Here, however, Helen Webb — a somewhat frail 82 year old — shrugged off the idea of evacuating to a community centre. Although her house temperature never rose above four degrees Celsius throughout the ordeal, she scoffed at rescue. At night, she slept bundled in socks and shoes, mitts and hat. During the day, she carefully picked her way across ice, taking up invitations from neighbours for hot drinks and barbecues. Though she would have been powerless to prevent it, her main reason for hanging in at home was to ensure her radiators didn't freeze and burst. She prided herself on being successful.

Chapter 8
The Pale Horse of Pestilence

Epidemic! *Contagion!* Both are fearsome words to Canadians, and to anyone else around the world. The sense of powerlessness these words instill in people can flay the human spirit as fiercely as a disease can ravage the flesh.

In the early 19th century, typhus was the greatest fear for settlers in Canada. Almost as prevalent as today's common cold, it was more deadly and less treatable. Typhus was transmitted by body lice, and it raged through the ships bringing immigrants to their new home. As such, the disease was primarily restricted to port cities such as Halifax and Quebec City.

However, things were about to get worse. Cholera — a far more deadly, far more contagious disease — was making its way to Canada. In response, in 1832 the government of

Lower Canada designated Grosse Île, a small island in the St. Lawrence River, as a quarantine station. Any inbound passengers or crew who were obviously sick or showing symptoms of illness were immediately quarantined. The seemingly healthy were allowed to proceed.

Unfortunately, medical science of the day did not understand the significance of incubation periods. As a result, Grosse Île and other small quarantine stations like it were woefully inadequate.

Cholera Comes Ashore

Despite preventive efforts, in 1832 cholera made it to Canada's shores. It wasn't airborne, and it wasn't transmitted from person to person. Instead, it was transmitted by sharing contaminated food and water. When cholera struck on the overcrowded ships and, later, in the overcrowded immigrant hostels and shanty sections of Lower and Upper Canada, its impact was compounded by its symptoms — loss of solids and fluids through copious amounts of uncontrollable diarrhea and vomiting. The results were severe: dehydration, organ failure, and then, for nearly 50 percent of those affected, death.

During the 1832 shipping season, more than 50,000 immigrants passed through Grosse Île. Of these, 40,000 made their way to Upper Canada. The first reported case of cholera in Canada arrived on April 28 on the ship *Constantia*, from Limerick. Twenty of the ship's passengers had already died at sea. For a time, the quarantine station seemed to be effective, but on June 8, Quebec City doctors reported the city's first case.

By June 16, the epidemic had made its way to Montreal. That day, a Montreal newspaper reported: "Business seems paralysed. Physicians and ministers in vehicles [travel] day and night through all parts of the city and suburbs; druggists and apothecaries keep their shops open all night. On Friday morning, the carts again appeared on the streets, bearing two or more coffins each, some with lids unfastened, and some corpses without coffins."

On June 18, the steamer *Great Britain* arrived in York (Toronto) carrying immigrants from the British Isles via Quebec City. After boarding the ship, York's medical officer, Dr. King, learned that a female passenger suffering from cholera had already been hospitalized in Kingston, while another in her last throes had been disembarked at Coburg. Moreover, two children had died on board, and two other people were showing early symptoms. The ship was held at York. In the following four weeks, 301 persons on board were diagnosed with cholera. Of these, 144 died.

As cholera swept through Upper Canada, people quickly learned it could invade any household. Within families it could also strike randomly, taking one parent but not another, one child but not a sibling.

By the end of the summer, the contagion was beginning to wane. Archdeacon John Strachan, a York civic leader, wrote that he was "just beginning to breathe from the cholera." In the same letter, he reflectively wrote, "York became a general hospital," a line that more than any other of the day described the disease's widespread impact.

Archdeacon Strachan went on to become an influential advocate for change in public health regulations. Even at the height of the epidemic, this was an uphill struggle. While the government in Britain had authorized the creation of local boards of health in Upper and Lower Canada, the boards were not provided with enforcement authority. They also didn't control their own budgets. At the time, local government funds were controlled by magistrates, lifetime appointees of colonial governors. Known collectively as the Family Compact, they had little interest in local affairs and approached their appointments as cushy jobs requiring no real work.

Despite the obstacles, the new boards of health did manage to push through court-ordered, binding regulations to combat the cholera, and those regulations were right on the mark, especially in York. Dr. King was empowered to board any vessel, without exception, that tried to land at York. Overcrowded houses and privies were ordered to be "limed" (lime being the common disinfectant of the times). Also, regular municipal garbage collection was ordered, footpaths were cleaned daily, and gutters were cleaned at least once weekly.

Although the regulations were in place, the York Board

of Health, among others, had to beg money from magistrates to implement the programs — a boondoggle that critically slowed response. This contributed to the animosity of settlers toward the Family Compact that eventually led to the Rebellion of 1837. Nevertheless, out of this political and social turmoil came a widespread acceptance that government had a responsibility and role in provision of preventive public health measures. In retrospect, this may have seemed minor, but it was the first building block of the health system Canadians have today.

The Return of Typhus
By 1847, Grosse Île was averaging 25,000 to 30,000 immigrants yearly, and was presumably ready for anything. However, it was not ready for the massive emigration of Irish during the 1845 to 1849 Irish Potato Famine, which reached its height in Canada in 1847, when 100,000 immigrants passed through Gross Île.

During the famine in Ireland, more than one million people had died, one-eighth of the population. Another one million emigrated, usually under the most horrendous conditions. Already suffering from severe malnutrition, those fleeing the country were crammed into unsanitary, lice-ridden steerage sections in the bowels of ships that were barely seaworthy.

The Darcy family was among the Irish emigrants of 1847. At the start of their voyage, the family included two parents, four daughters, and four sons. During the journey, however, a son, two daughters, and their mother all perished from typhus. Soon after, two more sons and the father died. The surviving daughters and son were adopted by a Quebecois family and grew up in Quebec's Eastern Townships. Their story was a typical one that year.

Grosse Île was not the only quarantine station overrun with the sick. A much smaller station on Middle Island in New Brunswick's Miramichi Bay consisted of little more than a few rundown fish-drying sheds. The area saw few immigrant ships until Joseph Cunard, founder of the Cunard Steamship Line, established a large shipyard nearby. Soon, Miramichi (named Chatham at the time) and neighbouring Newcastle became attractive immigrant destinations.

The immigrant ship *Looshtauk* was no Cunard liner. In June 1847, when it arrived at Middle Island from Cork, it was near-derelict. Almost the entire crew and complement of passengers were sick with typhus. Dr. James Brody, assigned to man the quarantine station, went aboard and found 117 passengers already dead and 300 others sick.

Soon, two more typhus-ridden ships arrived. Brody was the only medical man at the station. Despite his exhaustion, and his horrendous working and living conditions, fearful townsfolk refused to allow him to leave the island. By the end of June, Brody had contracted the disease himself. In early July, he died. He was only 28 years old.

During this typhus outbreak, more than 5000 people

died at sea and, at Grosse Île, officials buried another 5500. Deaths at Montreal and Kingston added to that total, as did those in the maritime and west coast ports.

The Spanish Flu Epidemic, Lest We Forget
Cholera and typhus were contained late in the 19th century, primarily as a result of improvements in public health. Years passed with no hint of widespread epidemics in Canada — until 1918.

That fall, Canadian soldiers began returning from the trenches of Europe. Finally, the Great War was winding down. However, the soldiers were coming from an infested wallow in which rats, decaying corpses, knee-high soupy mud, and barely edible rations were commonplace. Along with these graphic memories, many also brought the Spanish influenza home.

The "flu," as the press of the day called it, likely originated in the Far East. Because of wartime censorship, the first reports of it had appeared in the neutral Spanish press, resulting in the name, Spanish influenza. In Canada, where everyone was exalting in the victorious conclusion of the war to end all wars, it suffocated celebration and strangled optimism.

Unlike cholera or typhus, exposure to unsanitary conditions was not a requisite for transmission of the flu. It was airborne. It didn't matter whether people were rich or poor, profane or virtuous — all were exposed. Its mild symptoms could also quickly escalate. In Montreal, two roommates went to bed, one complaining of a sniffle. The next morning, the sniffler was dead.

On October 16, the mayor of Saskatoon, MacGregor Young, stated that "there is no cause for alarm." The next day he closed the city. Public meetings were banned. Schools, churches, theatres, even pool halls and bowling alleys were ordered closed. These actions were typical in towns and cities across the country.

Joseph Alexander enlisted in the Royal Newfoundland Regiment, perfectly fit, on October 18. Two days later, he joined a sick parade. Four days later, he was dead. Will Bird and his friend, Tommy, had spent two years in the trenches. Safe now, far removed from the battlefield, Tommy said he felt feverish around noon one day. Late that afternoon, he was admitted to hospital. By the next morning he was dead.

Death carts rattled through every street in Canada. Those who lived could only tend to the sick and dying and wait for the carts to stop at their doors. Undertakers ran out of coffins. The dead had to be stored in warehouses and community centres. In the Far North, the ground was too frozen to dig graves, so bodies were put on roofs to keep them from the dogs until spring.

In the U.S., the story was the same. The death toll from the flu was nearly 700,000, far more than that of the Civil War and Great Wars combined. In Canada, the number of deaths was estimated at 50,000.

Fatalities were highest among people between 20 and 40 years old. The death rate among those afflicted was about 20 percent. There was no cure for the flu other than the relief that could be offered by home remedies and nostrums — plasters and poultices of mustard, garlic, camphor, mint, cloves, and Epsom salts.

Nonetheless, people tried whatever they could in the hopes that something might work. In Saskatchewan's Mayfair district, as Teresa Bishop recounted, the local doctor prescribed that sliced onions be placed about a house, then burned after a few days and replaced with new onions. "If the onions did it or not, we will never know, but we did not get the flu."

Mrs. Maloney, the boarding house cook for employees at the Government of Canada's Lethbridge Research Farm, insisted all food be cooked and all water boiled. She gained local cachet when only one of her boarders took ill, a truck driver who occasionally took his meals in town.

The wearing of face masks, later proven to be ineffective, became law in many locales. Failure to wear one in public could bring a fine, although penalties in Canada were not as severe as those in New York City, where the crime could bring a $500 fine and a year in jail.

Chewing tobacco lost its popularity when public spitting was banned. Reporting on the situation in Montreal, the *Halifax Herald* noted that on October 12, 1918, 20 men were found guilty of spitting on the sidewalk and were sentenced up to $15 and a month in jail. On the same day, Montreal reported 20,000 known cases of flu in the city, with doctors reporting 600 new cases for that day alone.

Businesses were quick to capitalize on the public's fears. The Dominion Life Assurance Company advertised flu insurance. The CCM Bicycle Company, Canada's largest manufacturer of bicycles, ran an ad campaign based on the virtue of fresh air and the avoidance of crowded public transit. Ironically, CCM had to cut back on bicycle production due to a shortage of workers caused by the flu.

Remote areas were also hard hit. In one Labrador village, only 59 of 266 inhabitants survived. In the small farming community of Rouleau, Saskatchewan, south of Regina, Prudence Roddy lost her father, mother, and one sister. Her nine-year-old brother, Cecil, was required to drive the family car into Rouleau to purchase food for the household.

The Spanish flu was the most horrific epidemic in Canadian history, made more so because it could not be prevented from spreading. As a result, it created tremendous fear, sometimes more incapacitating than the epidemic itself. Knowing their vulnerability, and powerless to change it, people could only wait for the pestilence — wait and hope it would not enter their homes.

Eventually, the epidemic waned. But for many survivors, it left an insidious vestige — guilt. So many people had died so randomly that survivors were faced with the question, "Why not me?" And there was no answer.

Summers of Sickness: Polio

The memory of each community's impotence in the face of the influenza epidemic led to major increases in public health resources throughout the country. Provincial governments began to fund construction of more hospitals and medical training facilities. Prevention became a watchword in the medical profession. No one wanted a repeat of 1918.

Despite this, the spectre of another epidemic coursed through Canada from 1935 to 1955, and again, medicine seemed unable to provide a defense. This time, the epidemic was paralytic poliomyelitis — polio. It was a crippler and a killer to which children were particularly susceptible.

It wasn't until the mid-1950s that polio could be prevented. For parents, before then, each spring and summer brought with them the fear that the disease would strike their children, at the very least leaving its mark on the rest of their lives. The worst year of all was 1953, with nearly 9000 cases reported across the country, almost double the previous year.

Polio rarely passed over those stricken in a few days and moved on. For some victims, those unable to breathe, doctors developed the iron lung. Patients could spend weeks or longer in these large metal tanks, motionless, with only their heads protruding. Other sufferers were strapped into cumbersome braces fashioned from heavy steel and leather thinly padded with foam, designed to immobilize affected arms and legs.

Margaret Clarke of Hamilton, Ontario, was stricken

when she was eight years old. At first she spent several weeks in an iron lung. Then, for five years she wore a steel brace extending from high on her chest to the bottom of one foot. She lost the use of one arm and wore a prosthetic shoe for the rest of her life.

Four-year old John Harris from Scarborough, Ontario, was hospitalized for seven months, and for the following two years wore a steel brace on one arm to immobilize it. At night he slept wearing a rigid leg brace that extended from his hip to the bottom of his foot. Doctors were also forced to carry out a tendon transplant on young John's hand to save its use — at the time a very radical treatment. A tendon in his ring finger was used to replace the tendon in his thumb to enable use of the critical opposing digit. The operation worked. With very little residual impairment, John went on to a successful family and professional life.

Fortunately, many children dramatically bounced back from the affliction, including two Canadian prime ministers, Jean Chrétien and Paul Martin Jr. National Hockey Hall of Famer Bill Gadsby was another survivor, along with well-known Canadian entertainers Donald Sutherland, Neil Young, and Joni Mitchell.

Typhus, cholera, smallpox, polio — all have been beaten back by medicine. Over the course, Canada's healthcare system has profoundly changed. As was recently demonstrated with the SARS outbreak, some potential epidemics can be contained. Others, however, may be just over the horizon.

Chapter 9
The Mississauga Miracle

The role of first responders is normally to secure the incident scene, provide immediate medical or rescue help if required, neutralize any immediate threat, identify and summon support, and provide crowd control. But how do these first responders cope knowing that a situation may instantly encompass an entire city, with the lives of hundreds of thousands of people relying on their judgment during the first few minutes of having arrived at an incident scene? Such an incident occurred in Mississauga, Ontario, in 1979.

For years leading up to the event, firefighters and other emergency personnel in southern Ontario had been aware that an accident with a truck, train, ship, or airplane —

especially in such a high-density population area — would have the potential to be a major disaster.

Mississauga, a city in its own right, is a quiet, prosperous bedroom suburb in Toronto's west end. Cutting through Mississauga is the main line of the Canadian Pacific Railway, an industrial artery along which thousands of litres of toxic industrial chemicals and other hazardous materials flow every day. One of Mississauga's main thoroughfares, Dundas Street, parallels the rail line almost all the way into downtown Toronto.

Around midnight on Saturday, November 10, 1979, near the intersection of Dundas and Mavis Streets in Mississauga, overheated wheel bearings and a snapped axle caused 23 cars of Canadian Pacific Railway Freight Train No. 54 to derail. Much of the 106-car train was made up of tanker cars carrying propane, chlorine in liquid and gas forms, styrene, toluene, and caustic soda.

The toxic power of chlorine gas was already well known. Its use as a weapon of war had killed thousands of soldiers during World War I and left many more maimed or weakened for life. Now, a leaking tank car containing 90 tons of liquid chlorine lay on its side, surrounded by the fiery wreckage of pressurized propane tank cars.

In the first moments after the derailment, trainman Larry Krupa may have saved the city and hundreds of thousands of other souls. He dashed from the engine into the superheated chaos and uncoupled the train from the derailed cars so that the balance of the tankers could be quickly driven to safety. As he worked, a nearby propane tank car exploded and launched into the air, landing nearly a kilometre away.

By the time firefighters arrived, the fire was already shooting 1500 metres into the night sky. Cyril Hare, one of the first to arrive, described his initial impression to the *Toronto Daily Star*: "When I arrived just before midnight, I thought many of us would not live through the night." Minutes later, as firefighters were still connecting hoses, another propane car exploded, knocking emergency personnel and onlookers flat and scattering hot metal shards over the accident scene. Luckily, no one was injured.

Some veterans of other chemical fires quickly recognized the smell of leaking chlorine gas. As its unmistakable stench thickened the air, its lethal danger increased. Firefighters knew that with the slightest shift in wind direction, the gas would engulf them. Most did not have respirators. Initially, some were not even aware of the peril they'd encountered. By the end, eight firefighters required treatment for chlorine poisoning and had to be monitored regularly for a decade after the disaster. Such are the insidious long-term effects of chlorine gas.

Mike Metcalfe was a first responder from the Mississauga Police Department. He was one of many who persevered throughout that long night, battling the inferno. An eight-year police veteran, he had already weathered several serious chemical- and gas-related explosions and fires, although never on this scale. Metcalfe stayed close to the fire line all night, moving with the firefighters and their equipment along the periphery of the blazing wreckage. Several times he dashed closer to the inferno to rescue firefighters overcome by fumes, assisting them back to emergency medical trailers. Metcalfe was later awarded the department's medal of bravery, and his career continued long after the incident. On January 1, 2004, he was appointed Mississauga's deputy chief of police.

Even before firefighters and police on the scene could fully assess the danger of the chemical soup blazing along the tracks, Mississauga Police Chief Doug Burrows, who had seen the explosions light up the sky, ordered the evacuation of nearby residences. Fire and police departments from other municipalities provided extra help. Burrows' action may initially have seemed precipitous, but at 1:30 a.m. when his department finally obtained the manifest of the train's contents, his command was proved fortuitous. The potential for disaster was enormous.

The first evacuation involved 1400 hospital patients. Throughout the pre-dawn hours, convoys of ambulances snaked in and out of Mississauga. Senior citizens' homes were evacuated, and police went door to door waking up residents. Occasionally, reluctant or disbelieving homeowners were brusquely told, "Get the hell out!"

By dawn, environment officials were on the scene. Mississauga's firefighters continued to work, washing down the fringes of the raging blaze and avoiding smoke and fumes as best they could. They knew that if the tank cars could not be cooled down, more explosions and gas dispersal were a certainty. With potential danger still hanging in the air, environment officials and the city's Emergency Measures Organization ordered an expanded evacuation.

Early on Sunday, emergency vehicles equipped with loudspeakers began patrolling Mississauga streets. By nightfall, more than 220,000 people had been evacuated, including some from the neighbouring city of Oakville. It was the largest and fastest organized evacuation in North American history to that date.

Along with police and emergency personnel, an unlikely group patrolled the deserted streets during daylight hours. These were technicians from a local chemical company monitoring levels of leaking chlorine and styrene because the two in combination with bright sunlight could produce mace. Indeed, in some sectors it already had, causing members of some clean-up crews to suffer severe, incapacitating irritation of their throats, eyes, and ears.

By Tuesday night, the firefighters' work was beginning to pay off — 150,000 people were permitted to return to their homes. On Wednesday, Ontario Humane Society volunteers were allowed into the still-endangered area to quickly feed house pets. By then, the fires had been extinguished. However, the chlorine continued to leak, and twice that day it spewed high into the air where, fortunately, it was picked up by a stiff southerly breeze and dispersed harmlessly over Lake Ontario.

At 8 p.m. on Friday, the last 33,000 residents were allowed to return to their homes. Ron and Kathleen Dabors were among the last to return. Ron's first task was to retrieve his car. The couple had been in their car waiting at the railway crossing when the derailment occurred. "As I was backing up," he said, "these tanker cars were following us down the road. I'll never forget the sight. There was this huge mushroom cloud. We thought we were going to be killed." Not only did Ron find his car intact where they'd abandoned it, still unlocked, but also his wife's new fur coat was still inside.

Not a single life had been lost in the Mississauga Miracle. Apart from the eight firefighters affected by the chlorine gas, only one other injury was reported — a broken leg suffered by a news cameraman who tripped and fell.

Afterword

Many times in a disaster the risk to rescuers is overshadowed by the plight of victims. The professionals who arrive first on the scene of disasters — police officers, firefighters, emergency medical workers, aircrews, sailors, draegermen — these are just workaday people who regularly, coolly face the same conditions as the victims, sometimes worse. Their work can be dangerous, thankless, and depressing. These people are not distinguished by fatefully being in a particular place at a particular time. In that sense they are not heroes. They do not look for medals or plaudits from the media. They are there because they expect no less from themselves, truly a high calling. And should they find themselves in the same plight as the victims, they expect no less from others.

Canada's Worst Disasters of the 20th Century

Year	Type of Disaster	Location	Fatalities
1902	Coal Creek mining explosion	Fernie, BC	128
1903	Frank Slide	Frank, AB	70
1906	Sinking of *Valencia*	Vancouver Island, BC	126
1907	Quebec Bridge collapse	Quebec City, QC	75
1910	Train collision	Spanish River, ON	63
1910	Rogers Pass avalanche	Revelstoke, BC	62
1914	Sinking of *Empress of Ireland*	Rimouski, QC	1,012
1914	Hillcrest Mine explosion	Hillcrest, BC	189
1914	*Noronic* fire	Toronto, ON	118
1917	Halifax explosion, ship collision	Halifax, NS	1,600
1917	Dominion Mine explosion	New Waterford, NS	65
1918	Spanish influenza	Nationwide	50,000
1918	Sinking of the *Princess Sophia*	Inside Passage, Alaska	343
1918	Sinking of *Florizel*	Cape Race, NF	94
1926	Laurier Palace Movie Theatre Fire	Montreal, QC	77
1936	Heat wave	Ontario & Manitoba	1,180
1942	Knights of Columbus hall fire	St. John's, NF	99
1954	Hurricane Hazel	Toronto, ON	81
1958	Springhill Mine collapse	Springhill, NS	75
1963	Trans-Canada Airlines crash	Ste. Therese, QC	118
1970	Air Canada crash	Toronto, ON	109
1982	Sinking of *Ocean Ranger*	Hibernia Field, NF	84
1985	Air India crash	Atlantic Ocean	*329
1998	Swissair crash	Peggy's Cove, NS	229

*Departure was from Canada and 280 passengers were Canadians.

Further Reading

Brown, R.G. *Blood on the Coal: The Story of Springhill Mining Disasters.* Windsor, N.S.: Lancelot Press, 1990.

Campbell, Lyall. *Sable Island Shipwrecks: Disaster and Survival at the North Atlantic Graveyard.* Halifax: Nimbus Publishing, 1940.

Coates, K. and Bill Morrison. *The Sinking of the Princess Sophia: Taking the North Down With Her.* Toronto: Oxford University Press, 1990.

Craig, John. *The Noronic Is Burning.* Toronto: General Publishing, 1976.

Grout, Derek. *Empress of Ireland: The Story of an Edwardian Liner.* London: Tempus Publishing, 2001.

Kennedy, Betty. *Hurricane Hazel.* Toronto: Macmillan, 1979.

Looker, Janet. *Disaster Canada.* Toronto: Lynx Images, 2000.

Middleton, William D. *The Bridge at Quebec.* Indiana University Press, 2001.

Report One: Royal Commission on the Ocean Ranger Disaster.
Ottawa: Canadian Government Publishing Centre, 1984.

Acknowledgments

Special thanks to the very helpful staff of the Ottawa Public Library, Rosemount Branch, and the National Library of Canada, who went out of their way to lead me through the stacks to just the right material for my purposes.

About the Author

Ottawa-based Art Montague also writes fiction, but his interests in history, biography, and crime remain constant. He is a professional member of Crime Writers of Canada and the Periodical Writers Association of Canada.

Art's first book for Altitude Publishing's Amazing Stories was *Canada's Rumrunners: Incredible Adventures and Exploits During Canada's Illicit Liquor Trade.*

OTHER AMAZING STORIES

These titles are available wherever you buy books. If you have trouble finding the book you want, call the Altitude order desk at **1-800-957-6888**, e-mail your request to: **orderdesk@altitudepublishing.com** or visit our Web site **at www.amazingstories.ca**

New **AMAZING STORIES** titles are published every month.

Comments on other *Amazing Stories* from readers & reviewers

"Tightly written volumes filled with lots of wit and humour about famous and infamous Canadians."
Eric Shackleton, *The Globe and Mail*

"The heightened sense of drama and intrigue, combined with a good dose of human interest is what sets Amazing Stories *apart."*
Pamela Klaffke, *Calgary Herald*

"This is popular history as it should be... For this price, buy two and give one to a friend."
Terry Cook, a reader from Ottawa, on **Rebel Women**

"Glasner creates the moment of the explosion itself in graphic detail...she builds detail upon gruesome detail to create a convincingly authentic picture."
Peggy McKinnon, *The Sunday Herald,* on **The Halifax Explosion**

"It was wonderful...I found I could not put it down. I was sorry when it was completed."
Dorothy F. from Manitoba on **Marie-Anne Lagimodière**

"Stories are rich in description, and bristle with a clever, stylish realness."
Mark Weber, *Central Alberta Advisor,* on **Ghost Town Stories II**

"A compelling read. Bertin...has selected only the most intriguing tales, which she narrates with a wealth of detail."
Joyce Glasner, *New Brunswick Reader,* on **Strange Events**

"The resulting book is one readers will want to share with all the women in their lives."
Lynn Martel, *Rocky Mountain Outlook,* on **Women Explorers**